Wordsmithing Your Way to Success
by Making Authors' Dreams Come True

The Nomad Editor

Living the Lifestyle You Want, Doing Work You Love

Tyler R. Tichelaar, PhD

The Nomad Editor:
Living the Lifestyle You Want, Doing Work You Love

Marquette Fiction
1202 Pine Street
Marquette, MI 49855
www.MarquetteFiction.com

Disclaimer: All references to clients in this book are fictional composites of client situations and do not reflect any specific client situation, except those where the client is directly named. In all other cases, client names have been changed to protect their privacy.

ISBN-13: 978-0-9962400-6-2

Library of Congress Control Number: 2018912514

Printed in the United States of America

Publication managed by Superior Book Productions,
www.SuperiorBookProductions.com

Interior Design and Layout: Larry Alexander

Illustrations: Kathy Kuczek, www.KathyKuczek.com

What Authors and Publishers Are Saying About
Tyler R. Tichelaar, Superior Book Productions,
and *The Nomad Editor*

"Wow! What an amazing service you provide! Your editorial expertise is a great investment for anyone who wants to become a best-selling author."
— Patrick Snow, Publishing Coach and International Best-Selling Author
of *Creating Your Own Destiny* and *Boy Entrepreneur*

"Tyler Tichelaar's inherent love of literature and his acumen at writing, as evidenced in his own excellent novels, has been vital in my development as a novice author. I had no idea the caliber of professional I was honored to meet when I signed on with Tyler R. Tichelaar, PhD. Tyler's wealth of knowledge of the industry and the business of self-publishing is also phenomenal, so he will always be my go-to man for whatever questions I have as a business person. He has surely found his calling; I am glad I have found *him!*"
— Mary Flinn, Author of
The One, Second Time's a Charm, and *Three Gifts*

"Tyler's proofreading for my quarterly publication is very thorough, prompt, and shows his mastery of the craft of writing. It has brought the quality of my magazine to a whole new level."
— Roslyn McGrath, Publisher of
Health & Happiness U.P. Magazine

"With an impressive knowledge of the English language, evidenced in his novels, Tichelaar is definitely top-notch. I ended up incorporating all his suggestions for revision and feel my book has profited tremendously as a result."
— Devin Dugan, Author of *Third*

"I just published my first book and couldn't have done it without Tyler. His turnaround time is fast, price is very reasonable, and most importantly, he cares. It is one thing to get the grammar and punctuation right. It is an entirely different thing to analyze and give valuable feedback on the content, flow, and humor. I was worried that he would get frustrated by my repetitive questions (i.e., what if we....). He was not. He made me feel like his only client, although I know he had a long line of projects waiting for him."
— Jeremy Kisner, CFP, CRPS, President, SureVest Capital Management,
and Author of *A Good Financial Advisor Will Tell You...*

"I highly recommend Superior Book Productions. I am a first-time author who self-published my book. Working with both Tyler and Larry [junior editor, interior book layout and cover designer, and web designer at Superior Book Productions] was an incredible experience. They took the lead and brought my manuscript to life. This was a huge process involving editing, interior book layout, creating a cover, building my website, and loading all my files for the e-book, hardcover, and paperback. The end result was nothing but incredible! I could not have done this without them. The timing of getting things done was right on schedule and the work was superb!"

— Alan Charles, Keynote Speaker—Drug Awareness and Prevention, Radio Host, and Author of *Walking Out the Other Side: An Addict's Journey from Loneliness to Life*

"While I have worked with other editors, Tyler and Larry of Superior Book Productions stand out. Their flexibility and on-time delivery makes working with them an exciting experience. As a returning customer, I can say with certainty that they provide flawless execution by not only editing grammar and punctuation, but the content to make sure there is a good flow of ideas from one section to the next. Tyler and Larry are not shy to redirect any author on the right path when things are not clear. I enjoyed working with them, and I will continue doing so in the future."

—Teddie E. Malangwasira, PhD and Author of *Leading in a Diverse Environment* and *Leadership Is Not About Race*

"I have worked with several editors, and I can safely say that Tyler Tichelaar is outstanding. He has a deep understanding of storytelling, language, and structure. Not only do I learn something every time we work together, but his feedback on story structure, characterization, and conversations helped me turn good books into great books."

— Chris Shockowitz, Author of the Zalthuras and Outward Bound series

"I had no idea how much I was getting when I brought my book to Tyler Tichelaar! Within twenty-four hours, I felt like he was my personal friend, who truly cared about *my book*! He is a magician when it comes to editing.... His services didn't stop once my book was published. (In fact, they still haven't!) When I think about the time he spent (still spends) with me...and the speed at which he responds, I can't fathom that he has other clients!"

— Carol Paul, Author of *Team Clean: The Ultimate Family Clean-Up-the-House Formula!*

"I had the good fortune to hire Tyler Tichelaar as my editor. Tyler guided me in transforming a bundle of thoughts into a flowing, readable book. He is an alchemist with words. He is a fun and enjoyable person to work with. He is skilled in taking difficult concepts and presenting them in a flowing, understandable format. Tyler's speed and accuracy are remarkable, and he keeps the project moving forward. Tyler is generous with his time and guided me in every aspect of the book. His generosity was also apparent in making his brilliant services affordable. Tyler is a literary genius and adds a golden dimension that is seamlessly woven into his work. I am so grateful to him for the magic he performed in editing my book."

— Fredrick Swaroop Honig, Author of
The Unitive Field: The Union of Science and Spirituality

"I found Superior Book Productions to be a most valuable partner in editing and producing my book, *The Essence of Lean*. This was my first book, and both Tyler and Larry were very helpful and responsive as they walked me through the entire process."

— David Hinds, PhD, Professor and Author of *The Essence of Lean*

"This was my first experience writing a book. As an editor, Tyler nurtured me, explaining the reason for any changes in the manuscript. He was so responsive that I felt he was always at my side ready to help, not only about wordsmithing, but also in navigating the intricacies of the publishing world. I could depend on him to answer my questions almost immediately even if they were sent during non-business hours. Larry was an easy transition for the interior design. He understood from the start my concept of how the book should appear. His experience in publishing and his expertise in formatting documents to required specifications were invaluable. My document was accepted immediately without the need for changes. I wholeheartedly recommend Superior Book Productions for any author wanting to get a book into print."

— Georgia Blair, Co-Author of
Banana George! Don't Wait for Life to Happen, Make It Happen

"I am indebted to the depth and acumen of Dr. Tichelaar's editorial skills."

— Victor R. Volkman, Owner of Loving Healing Press

To Vaughn,
Who gave me the idea to write this book.

Acknowledgments

I<span></span>T WOULD HAVE been impossible to write this book if I didn't have editing clients and people who believed in me enough to help me become an editor. I wish to thank in particular:

Vaughn Laurila, who first gave me the idea to write this book. He has brainstormed business ideas and shared books with me for over a decade. I appreciate how he has always supported and helped to enhance my dreams.

Patrick Snow was the first person who sent me books to edit from his publishing clients. Without his support, I might never have become an editor. I remain indebted to him for a lifetime. We make a great team.

Alex Kofsky helped me come up with the title for this book and coached me through the final stages to create a truly marketable product. He is an old soul, wise beyond his years.

Irene Watson helped me to become self-employed by hiring me as a book reviewer for Reader Views and then to write press releases, interview authors, and edit books for her clients. Irene, you are gone but not forgotten. When faced with a challenge, I constantly think, "What would Irene do?"

Victor Volkman, along with Irene Watson, first interviewed me on the *Authors Access* internet radio show. Next thing I knew, I was a guest cohost. As time went by, Victor and I became board members together for the Upper Peninsula Publishers and Authors Association, he published some of my books through Modern History Press, and he continues to use my editing services as well as offer me advice. His support has been invaluable.

Pat Ryan O'Day hired me to be the proofreader at *Marquette Monthly* where I was able to polish my editing and proofreading skills under someone who had been in the magazine business for decades. Pat, I know you're up there smiling about how many people, like myself, are still benefiting from your influence.

Larry Alexander is more like my brother than my business colleague. Since we first shared an office and taught composition at Northern Michigan University more than a quarter century ago, we have been friends. He has selflessly supported my writing and self-employment goals and become part of my team. I thank him for his own incredible editing skills and for the stellar layout and design of this and all my books. Larry, you are my rock.

Kathy Kuczek's fabulous illustrations far exceeded my expectations and gave the tone and feel to the book I wanted. Her work proves that a picture is worth a thousand words.

Diana Deluca, Roslyn Hurley, and Jenifer Brady all read early drafts of the book and provided me with insightful feedback and support. They are the best beta readers an author—and an editor—could wish for. They are also wonderful, longtime friends.

To my many English teachers and professors: I appreciate what all of you taught me, especially when you corrected my errors. It was no fun getting an A for content and an F for grammar on my papers, but it made me learn grammar and punctuation—a gift you gave me that I'm now giving to others.

My editing clients are far too many to mention, but they have all helped me to live my dream. I feel privileged to have also been able to play a role in the achievement of theirs. Thank you. It's been a joy to serve you.

Contents

Foreword
by Patrick Snow

WHEN I BEGAN my career some twenty-five years ago as a new author and speaker, I was clueless about the importance of editing and how a good editor can make or break a book's success. I stumbled across a few editors here and there, but I had no real success with them. As a result, the first printing of my book *Creating Your Own Destiny* had more than fifty grammar and spelling errors. I soon found myself embarrassed and looking for a new editor.

Then I began to ask myself, "How and where can I find an editor who can make my words shine, get my point across, and deliver a professional piece of work to the marketplace?" I remained dumbfounded—there just seemed to be so many editing options out there, but how could I know whom to trust, whether they were any good, or even if they were overcharging me? Plus, what was a reasonable time to get my manuscript reedited and turned into a product I could be proud of?

I quickly discovered all editors are not the same! Some are just in it for the money, while others take ownership of their clients' work, are passionate about quality, and seek to communicate the author's voice to the reader. I finally understood the difference between copy editing, content editing, hybrid ghostwriting, and full ghostwriting. And it was Tyler Tichelaar who taught me all of this, and so much more.

In 2007, I had the opportunity to be the keynote speaker for the Upper Peninsula Publishers and Authors Association's annual meeting in Marquette, Michigan. There I had the pleasure of meeting Tyler for the first time. We soon became great friends; he reedited *Creating Your Own Destiny*, eliminating all the errors in my book, retaining my voice, and altogether making my book shine. Since then, Tyler has edited all of my other books and countless special reports.

After that, Tyler and I formed a business partnership. He has become the managing editor for my publishing coaching business, which has successfully produced upwards of 1,200 books for my clients in the last twenty years. Tyler has edited and proofread hundreds of those books. He has also traveled to both Maui, Hawaii, and Seattle, Washington, to speak at my Best Seller Publishing Institutes and is a regular and sought-after guest instructor on my weekly Inner Circle coaching calls.

I consistently hear rave reviews from my clients about the quality of Tyler's work. I will probably embarrass him with these comments, but I am convinced that Tyler Tichelaar is one of the great writers and editors of our time. His difference is that he cares about authors, and he can deliver a higher quality to the marketplace than anyone else I have ever met. He once took a terrible, sixty-five-page manuscript from an older client of mine in her seventies who barely spoke English as her third language, overhauled it, did a complete hybrid ghostwrite, and delivered a world-class, 175-page book that made the woman look like she had mastered the English language. I have 100 other stories about Tyler Tichelaar just like this that have literally allowed my clients to use the books he has edited for them to quit their jobs and earn full-time livings as authors, speakers, and coaches.

In *The Nomad Editor*, Tyler Tichelaar will show you exactly how to achieve your dreams, working from home, doing the work you love, while serving others. In the process, he will teach you how to gain control of your life, your career, and your writing passions.

Furthermore, when you follow the formulas and strategies in this book, you will acquire the basic skills and knowledge needed to succeed as an editor. You will learn how much to charge, how and when to accept payment, and how to set up your business working from home. You will learn how to market yourself and your business to attract paying clientele. Most importantly, you will learn how to deliver value to your clients so they will become your lifetime fans, and you will then receive years and years of warm referrals from your happy and successful clients. Additionally, you will learn how to avoid the clients who will eat you alive by stealing all your time. You will learn how to juggle multiple projects, meet deadlines, and grow your business in such a way that you will never have to punch a time clock for a job or work for someone else again. Tyler Tichelaar is absolutely brilliant and provides you with a complete turnkey editing business in a box, except it is written and communicated to you in a book. *The Nomad Editor* is perhaps the most important resource you will ever need to succeed in this space, and I am sure one day it will be considered the single greatest resource book editors need to ensure their success!

Reading this book and applying it to your life and business will enable you to live the life you have already dreamed about; you will succeed at working from home as a successful editor serving hundreds of clients on a global basis. Tyler has been building his business on multiple continents and has clients as far away as Australia and New Zealand, and all of them sing his praises. You, too, can experience this level of success when you apply his wisdom and insights to your editing business.

Throughout this book, you will learn that you are the driving force needed to build the business you desire. You have the power, skill set, and determination to succeed, but you will only achieve this success when you read, reread, and apply these insights to your life and business. Tyler will show you the importance of being nice, showing empathy, and doing research for clients so their messages are historically accurate, all their quotes are correctly attributed, and so forth.

The marvelous thing about Tyler is that he is not just an editor. He is also a proofreader and a successful book reviewer. Many of the book reviews he has written have been so successful that they have landed my clients on national media programs such as Fox News and in newspapers like the *Seattle Post-Intelligencer*.

Tyler's academic credentials include a PhD in literature from Western Michigan University, and master's and bachelor's degrees in English from Northern Michigan University. More importantly, he is an award-winning author of twenty books, ranging from historical fiction and fantasy to literary criticism and biography. His talent is off the charts, and I personally believe his books are right up there with those of Mark Twain, Edgar Allan Poe, Charles Dickens, and other greats! He is every bit the talent they are, and arguably their modern version!

The bottom line is this: If you want to be a successful editor, then Tyler Tichelaar is your man, and this is your book. So get ready for an amazing ride. Put up your tray table, fasten your seatbelt, and hold on for the journey of a lifetime. Your future begins now, and your dreams are about to come true. Mark my words!

Enjoy your journey of serving others, and financially benefitting for a lifetime as a result. I believe in you. Tyler believes in you. We know when you apply the wisdom in these pages, you will become an unstoppable force, fully capable of creating your own destiny!

Respectfully,

Patrick Snow

Publishing and Book Marketing Coach and International Best-Selling Author of *Creating Your Own Destiny*, *The Affluent Entrepreneur*, and *Boy Entrepreneur*

www.PatrickSnow.com
www.ThePublishingDoctor.com

Introduction

> "Blessed is he who has found his work; let him ask no other blessedness.
> He has a work, a life-purpose; he has found it, and will follow it!"
>
> — Thomas Carlyle, *Past and Present*

D O YOU LOVE books? Can you pay close attention to detail? Do you have strong writing skills and a firm grasp of grammar and punctuation rules?

Then you might have the skills to become an editor.

Are you tired of having your talents overlooked? Are you tired of fighting traffic on your daily commute? Do you want the flexibility to go to lunch with friends or take a day off when you wish? Would you like to travel when and where you want and still be able to work wherever you are?

Then you may enjoy becoming a freelancer.

Are you able to set, achieve, and surpass daily goals? Are you able to juggle multiple projects at once? Can you abide by your word, meet deadlines, and provide high quality work?

Then you may have the motivation to be a business owner.

I decided to write *The Nomad Editor* because many people over the years have asked me how to become a freelance editor and work from home—or wherever in the world they want. I also have had many would-be editors ask me to hire them. Some of them had the skills, some did not.

Here's the thing: No degree programs exist for how to become an editor. There is no required course of study, and there is no universally recognized certification to determine whether you are qualified. I'm afraid the grammar police don't have any real authority.

A lot of people think they have what it takes to be an editor. I can't tell you how many books I have had to rescue after authors told me they already had their books edited by "my niece who is an English major," "my sister who is a librarian," or "my friend who writes real good." Chances are none of those people had the required skills to be an editor, especially not a book editor. And the authors who hired them had no clue their editors weren't up to snuff since they didn't have excellent writing skills themselves. After all, some think their friends "write *real good.*" Ugh.

Am I qualified to be an editor? I believe I am because of my education and years of experience, but in the beginning, even I wasn't so sure. If you're starting to feel a bit of doubt right now about whether you have what it takes to be an editor, that's probably a good sign that you might be more qualified than many who think they are editors and really aren't. It shows you have a conscious and are conscientious. Rest assured, even if you don't have the skills, you can get them.

You wouldn't be reading this book if you weren't interested in becoming a freelance editor. Hopefully, I can help you along on that journey. I'll admit upfront, however, that I won't have all the answers for you. I'm still learning myself. Sadly, there are scarce resources for those who wish to become editors. There are a few workshops or summer programs you might attend, but even those aren't the same as in-the-field experience. As a result, I'm largely self-taught, although I believe years of school, writing for publication, and teaching writing at the college level ultimately prepared me for the work I do today.

In these pages, I will share how I became an editor and how I remain one by keeping my business growing and lucrative. You'll learn about the technical skills you need, but because grammar and punctuation can be learned elsewhere—and hopefully you already have mastered them—this book will focus upon an editor's daily life. You'll learn about the other skills I use every day, such as time management, customer service, record-keeping, marketing, and sales. You'll acquire tools for dealing with difficult clients and for meeting deadlines without having to work long hours. You'll learn a little about how the publishing industry works, and you'll discover how to set boundaries between your work and your personal life so you don't lose your sanity. Ultimately, you will be prepared to achieve success. You might even get a few good chuckles from my experiences.

Are you ready to begin? Then I have a test for you. In this chapter there was a typo. Did you catch it? If so, congratulations. If not, go back and look for it. (Hopefully, you won't find any I left there by accident—nothing's more embarrassing as an editor than being told you missed a typo, but it does happen.) So did you find that typo? Three paragraphs back, the word *conscious* was used when *conscience* should have been. If you caught it, I suspect you may have what it takes to be an editor, at least when it comes to paying attention to detail.

Do you have a thick skin? That's definitely another requirement. You need to be a perfectionist who won't beat yourself up over an error when it happens, and you have to be prepared not to let your clients beat you up over them either. So if you missed that typo, don't feel too bad. So far, I've edited more than 400 books, and no one has chewed me out over a typo yet, but now and then, I hate to admit it, someone does catch one I missed.

But there's more to editing than just catching typos. There are many skills you will need to succeed, so let's start looking at those skills and what your life as an editor will look like.

I wish you much success in the pursuit of your career. May your Wi-Fi never fail you as you travel the world editing books. May all your subjects and pronouns agree. And may you find joy in helping to add life-changing books to the world.

Here's to your good fortune!

Tyler R. Tichelaar

Chapter 1
My Nomadic Journey to Editing

"Sitting alone in a room reading a book, with no one to interrupt me.
That is all I ever consciously wanted out of life."

— Anne Tyler, *Celestial Navigation*

I WAS BORN ON Wednesday, May 26, 1971, in St. Luke's Hospital (later known as Marquette General Hospital and today as UP Health System) in Marquette, Michigan, at 4:11 p.m. to Richard and Nancy (nee White) Tichelaar.

Why do I start off with such a detailed, boring, "who cares" sentence? As an example of what you have to watch out for and correct when you are an editor. This book is not my biography but a book about editing, so this chapter should only contain facts relevant to my topic. As an editor, you need to know how to cut, cut, cut anything that does not relate to the topic's purpose or advance the plot. (Even if you are editing nonfiction, there is a plot, or purpose, the book is moving toward; we'll talk more about that in Chapter 13.) Never be afraid to cut what falls under the umbrella of boring and irrelevant.

So let me begin again, this time only incorporating what is relevant to understanding my background as it relates to becoming an editor.

I never considered the possibility of being an editor until I was in my early thirties. Like most freelance editors out there, I'd already had a few different careers before I found my true vocation. But from an early age, my interests and occupations were preparing me for eventually becoming a full-time freelance editor, which I did when I was thirty-seven.

Of course, I was the kid who always had his nose in a book. I loved to read. Not only that, but I also loved to write. In grade school, I would staple pieces of paper together to make my own books and then copy stories out of other books or write my own. I still have the books I made in third grade in Young Authors.

In fourth grade, one of my friends told me she had an aunt who was an author. That's when it dawned on me that being an author was a job. And that was the job I wanted.

I doubt I had even heard the word "editor" at that age.

I set my goal on becoming an author. When I told people that was my dream, many of them told me how hard it would be to make it a reality. I took that as a challenge and remained determined. I became the weird kid reading Dickens and Jane Austen in high school. I wanted to learn how to be the best author possible, and I believed I could only do that by studying master novelists.

After a few false writing attempts, including an entire sequel to *Gone with the Wind* that I wrote in my head, I began on June 4, 1987, to pen what would be the first novel I would complete. I was sixteen and very dedicated to my craft, sitting at my desk for two hours every morning during summer vacation until I had a complete draft. Then I revised it multiple times—all by hand. I finished my novel in two years, and then, when I was eighteen and had started college, I typed it all on my first computer.

In the fall of 1989, I began college at Northern Michigan University in my hometown of Marquette. College limited the time I had to write novels, but it also allowed me to learn more about my craft. Of course, I became an English major. Specifically, I was in the graduate-bound program. That meant lots of literature courses, and I took more than necessary: Shakespeare, Chaucer, British and American literature surveys, major authors courses in James Joyce and William Wordsworth and Samuel Taylor Coleridge. I also took creative writing classes and continued to write.

My goal in college was to publish my first novel so that when I graduated, I would be prepared to live the life of an author, always writing and living off my royalties. That dream was exposed to reality when, in the spring of 1991, I sent my first novel off to a publisher. After a few weeks, the editor at the publishing company wrote back praising my manuscript but telling me the company had just bought two other novels, so would I be willing to share in the publishing costs? My share of those costs would be many thousands of dollars. At that time, I was working at McDonald's for $3.35 an hour. Obviously, I said no.

Suffice to say, I didn't get a novel published while I was in college. I kept sending my first novel out, and I collected rejection letters, but I also managed to write two more novels during those years. My junior and senior years, I got a job working at the Writing Center on campus. That was my first real experience with editing. I read students' papers, marked them up, and then gave the students suggestions for improvement. I loved doing it, but the thought of becoming an editor never occurred to me. My senior year, I had no idea what I would do with my bachelor's in English, so I decided I would get a master's degree. I went to the English department secretary and asked for an application for the MA program. She asked whether I also wanted one for becoming a teaching assistant. I had no idea the English department even had teaching assistants, but I said yes. After all, I was told it would pay $4,500 a year. That was better than what I had been making at McDonald's or the Writing Center.

I had no teaching experience, but since I had worked at the Writing Center and been named the Outstanding Senior in the English Department, I got my foot in the door and soon had twenty-four freshman to teach how to write essays. I turned out to be a fairly good teacher—not fabulous, but I liked teaching and my students seemed to like me. I realized I could make a small difference in the world by teaching and encouraging students to have dreams, think for themselves, and learn how to communicate their ideas.

Meanwhile, my dream of being an author continued. By then, I was old enough to know how the real world worked, so I became more practical, deciding I would continue teaching to support myself until I got a book published and could start collecting those royalties.

In the spring of 1995, I was accepted into the doctorate program at Western Michigan University, in Kalamazoo. Kalamazoo was about 465 miles from my hometown of Marquette, so I was reluctant to move so far. I committed to being at Western in the autumn, but in my heart, I had some questions about moving so far from my family and friends. That summer, I signed up to do temporary work with Manpower. I was sent to work for Lutheran Social Services, where I typed up adoption records and other documents that had been voice-recorded. I was a fairly fast typist, and I also got the punctuation and grammar right, which not all the people the agency hired could do. I learned a valuable lesson at Manpower. If you are paid hourly and you are fast, you will quickly work your way out of a job. In other words, if I could do in fifteen hours what someone else could do in twenty, and we were both being paid $7.00 an hour, then I would ultimately make $105, and the other person would make $140, even though I got the job done faster. I have never in my life slacked off on a job, and I will always do the job as quickly and accurately as possible, but I learned a valuable lesson about the need to ensure you are paid what you are worth.

I did go to Western Michigan University, and five years later, I had earned a PhD in literature with a specialty in nineteenth century British literature. I wrote my dissertation on Gothic literature, which was later published in 2012 as *The Gothic Wanderer: From Transgression to Redemption* by Modern History Press. During my years at Western, I taught freshman composition, British literature, and co-taught classes in post-colonial literature and James Joyce. I loved teaching and I loved studying literature, and most of the time, I loved my students. Grading their papers wasn't always fun, especially when they didn't take the class seriously, but I did my best to help them become better writers. Grading papers is excellent practice for editing books—books are just about fifty times longer. By that point, I was also trying to get scholarly articles published in journals so I was starting to work with editors, but becoming an editor myself still never dawned on me.

As I neared completion of my doctorate, I began looking for a teaching job at the university level—ideally, the perfect tenure-track position in which I would teach nineteenth century British literature. However, a few hundred other people had just graduated with doctorates in British literature, and they were all looking for jobs, so there just weren't enough positions to go around. After I applied for 200 positions, and collected 200 rejection letters, I was finally offered a one-year position, renewable for four years, at Clemson University in South Carolina—even farther from home! The pay wasn't very good, but it was better than being an adjunct at Western Michigan University or Northern Michigan University, the only other options open to me. At Clemson, I would teach four classes each semester, earning $24,000 annually. If I had been an adjunct at Western or Northern, I would have gotten $3,000 for one class, so being at Clemson was equivalent to having four adjunct positions—a ton of work, but enough money to live on—barely.

At Clemson, I taught three sections of freshman composition and one section of the British literature survey. Of course, teaching composition meant grading tons of papers. It was standard to assign about six papers per course, and with about twenty-four students per class, that meant grading 432 four- to five-page papers each semester, and that didn't count grading the British literature quizzes and papers. It may be called grading papers, but it's really editing. My students turned in their essays on paper, and I then corrected them, inserting commas, marking misspellings, and pointing out where they should rewrite sentences, expand content, or cut unnecessary details. Students were expected to revise a few of their papers for their portfolios, so it was very much an editing and revising process. If you want to be an editor, try teaching first. Grading papers can be a hair-pulling experience, but it will teach you what to expect from writers and how to teach them to improve their writing.

Because I wish to be as truthful as possible in this book about what you will face as an editor, let me say this: Many of the authors I work with write no better than my college freshmen did. Some of them write worse because they've been out of college for so long and have not needed to write much in their careers. That isn't to say I didn't have some really good writers among my students, and equally, I work with some really good authors, but the percentage of good to poor writers is about the same as among college freshmen.

All that said, I enjoyed teaching. I loved teaching literature. I loved freshman composition too when my students applied themselves and I actually saw them improve over the course of the semester. But I was also frustrated by those who made no effort but just kept turning in the same poor quality work that made me suspect they had written their papers the night before and only as one draft.

I would have continued teaching, despite my students' lack of effort, if only to pay the bills, except that Clemson was 1,200 miles from Marquette, and my heart was in Marquette. I continued to apply for better teaching positions without success, and then mid-year, the State of South Carolina needed to cut half-a-billion dollars from its budget, and that meant all the state universities needed to make budget cuts. You guessed it—there went my job. Without any other job prospects, I decided I would move back to Marquette. I didn't want to keep moving from one university to another for years while trying to get that elusive tenure-track position. I also was used to cooler temperatures and South Carolina was already far too hot, so I didn't want to end up at a school in Texas or Arizona. In the end, Clemson came up with the money for me to return the following year, but by the spring of 2001, I had decided I needed to go home.

I was still writing novels during this time. In fact, in 1999, I began writing a novel that would eventually become The Marquette Trilogy, a historical fiction series about my hometown. While at Clemson, I kept trying to write scholarly papers to submit to journals, but my interest in doing so quickly waned. Journals paid nothing for articles, and even if I got my articles published, they would only be read by the hundred or so specialists in my field. The only reason to write them seemed to be to get noticed so you'd get tenure. I was disillusioned by academia at this point. I mean, how many people besides me really cared about the Wandering Jew theme as expressed in Fanny Burney's 1814 novel *The Wanderer*, or Dickens' use of Rosicrucianism in *A Tale of Two Cities*? No, I would rather write novels and reach a wider audience. In writing my trilogy, I had decided it was time Upper Michigan was depicted in adult fiction and its importance made known to the world. Up to that point, only a few novels, such as Robert Traver's *An Anatomy of a Murder*, had been set in Upper Michigan. I wanted to help create a literature for Upper Michigan. My purpose became to—perhaps a bit arrogantly—as Stephen Dedalus writes in James Joyce's *A Portrait of the Artist as a Young Man*, "forge in the smithy of my soul the uncreated conscience of my race." To do that, I felt I had to be in Marquette. And so I took a leap of faith, left academia, and returned home.

I wish I could say I published a book right after I moved back to Marquette and it was all smooth sailing from then on, but life rarely works like that. I moved back in with my parents and spent that summer applying for jobs locally and writing my novels. I had no idea initially that the one novel I planned to write would turn into a trilogy, or that it would take two years of basically just doing research on Marquette's history and three more years of writing to complete it, but I dedicated myself to the task and wrote religiously every evening and for many hours on weekends.

Meanwhile, no employer in Marquette wanted to give me a job. All the people who interviewed me suspected I was just waiting to be hired at Northern Michigan University, and once that happened, I would quit, even though I explained to them that there were no teaching jobs at NMU for me. Ultimately, I ended up working for Manpower again, doing temporary work in a lawyer's office, until I finally landed a full-time job with health benefits at a call center. Full-time and health benefits sound good, but the job paid $7.50 an hour and consisted of answering the phone. I was mostly taking phone calls for a gas and electricity supplier, and it was a rare day when I didn't get sworn at by a customer angry about a bill. I even had a customer threaten to come to my office and "take me out." This employment situation was a far cry from what I went to school for, and more than a 33 percent pay cut from the low wages I had been making at Clemson. But it was a job, and I was back home, and I still hoped to get a novel published and fulfill what I believed was my destiny.

By 2003, I was still at the call center after nearly two years, still unsuccessfully trying to find a better job and coming to the conclusion that I would be better off moving to a larger city. I knew I didn't want to go back into teaching because of the job market, and I would no longer be even remotely competitive because I had been out of academia for two years. Only then did I consider I might become an editor and work for a publishing house in New

York, or, preferably, Chicago, which was closer to Marquette. But I hated big cities, so I kept dragging my feet about moving.

Then, in April 2003, I was promoted to call center supervisor. It was a significant raise—about as much money as I had made at Clemson. It was also closer to the kind of role I was used to since being a manager is in many ways like being a teacher; you have to train and manage employees, just like you do students. I still had to talk to the most difficult customers when they got mad at my employees, but I didn't have to talk to customers eight hours a day. After another year, I was promoted to call center manager, which was even better. I was now part of the management team and making a decent enough wage that I was able to buy a house. I also was able to use my education a little in writing some marketing pieces for the company. That was the best part of my job.

Trust me, I could write a whole book about working in a call center. It was a lot like the antics on the TV show *The Office*. Someday, I will write a comical novel about it. What's important, however, is that I was able to find a job to tide me over while I continued working toward my dream of becoming an author.

Finally, in 2004, I had finished writing my trilogy and begun looking for a publisher. Meanwhile, I wrote two more novels. I sent out query letters to publishers and agents, and I began to collect rejection letters. A few of the rejection letters were actually personalized rather than being just form letters. The editors said how much they would like to help with the project, but they thought my novels were too regional or just not the right fit for them. I could understand that. Publishers in New York knew nothing about Upper Michigan, and they couldn't see how readers across the nation would be interested in reading about it, even though I tried to convince them that my novels reflected the American Dream playing out in a city that could be a microcosm for any in the United States, and, therefore, it would resonate with readers nationwide. Regardless, the publishers just didn't have the vision I had for my novels.

I continued to send out letters to publishers, and I continued to collect rejection letters, until one day I had an epiphany. "Why," I asked myself, "should someone in New York get to decide whether people in Upper Michigan are allowed to read my books?" What I had been doing made no sense. It was time to take control of the situation. It was time to figure out how I could publish my novels myself.

About this time, the self-publishing revolution was beginning. Improvements in technology meant that books could be printed on demand. The result was a steep decline in book production costs. In the 1980s, I had heard stories of people who had spent $30,000 to self-publish a book. After a little research, I discovered I could publish a book with an online print-on-demand company for as little as $1,000. The print-on-demand publisher would do the interior layout, design the cover for me, and give me twenty copies for that price. It would even do an editorial evaluation. I couldn't have found a better deal. I could also buy copies from the publisher at a significant discount. (Later, I would discover that discount wasn't significant enough—the local bookstores wanted 40 percent of my sales, which meant I would lose eight cents for every book I sold in a bookstore. As a result, I would seek out even more inexpensive ways to publish my successive books. But for the time being, I had found a way to print my books in an affordable manner and begin to sell them to my prospective readers in Upper Michigan.)

My purpose here isn't to explain self-publishing. Plenty of books have been written on the topic, and I recommend that anyone interested in being a freelance editor read some of them; you'll want to learn all aspects of the publishing industry so you can make life easier for your clients who will need handholding and expect you not only to be their editor but their publishing coach; you'll also want to learn how to work with layout people and printers to make your clients' books look professional and to make the jobs of everyone involved easier. *Dan Poynter's Self-Publishing Manual* is a great book to start with.

The important thing is that I took another leap of faith and published my first novel, *Iron Pioneers: The Marquette Trilogy, Book One*, in February 2006. It wasn't an overnight success, but it got enough local interest that I made back my expenses and went on to publish the next two novels in the trilogy, and then several more books as the years went by. With the publication of this book, I am now the author of twenty books, and I plan to write and publish many more before I'm done.

Once I had self-published, I discovered I also had to learn about marketing if I was going to get anyone to read my books. Many authors find marketing to be their biggest obstacle because they are introverts; they want to write their books, but they don't want to speak in public about them or try to convince anyone to buy them. I don't pretend to be a great marketer, but I've never shied away from it, even when it's meant forcing myself to pick up the phone or go into a bookstore to talk to the manager. When I was about to publish my first book, I realized, "If I can sell gas and electricity—which I don't care about—to people over the phone for eight hours a day, then I can definitely sell my books, which I really care about."

Today, as a freelance editor, I also have to know how to market my services to people, and so being a salesperson in a call center, as much as I disliked the job, ended up benefiting me in multiple ways in the long run.

My life now started to change dramatically. I thought by publishing my first book, I was launching my career as an author, and I was, but I was also on the brink of launching my career as an editor. This change came about through a mix of good fortune and a strong determination to find a new career that would be fulfilling and allow me to use my education.

Soon after I published my first book, I joined the Upper Peninsula Publishers and Authors Association. Through that organization, and mainly by talking to the other members, I learned a lot about self-publishing and book marketing. At about the same time, the company I worked for was in a bad position due to efforts to overturn deregulation in Michigan. I was concerned I might lose my job, and I was also unhappy wasting my writing skills and education, so I began looking for other sources of income. I knew it was unlikely I could support myself on book sales alone—since by now I had accepted that my regional novels were unlikely to become national bestsellers— and I knew there were no jobs in Marquette conducive to what I wanted to do. I didn't want to go back into teaching, and I was tired of working for other people I didn't always see eye-to-eye with, so I started looking online for work that would involve writing—work I could do from home. I joined self-publishing listservs, posted book reviews to Amazon, and did anything else I could think of to get noticed and find other sources of income connected to writing. Through this hit-and-miss search for a new career, I eventually became an editor. For about a year, I felt frustrated over my inability to find fulfilling work, and then everything came together very quickly.

One day, I responded to an email request for authors to be interviewed for the *Authors Access* internet radio show. I suggested I could speak on the show about writing regional fiction. The show's hosts, Irene Watson and Victor Volkman, agreed to have me on the program. Little did I know they would soon become two of my best friends in the publishing industry. Irene owned Reader Views, a book review and publicity company, and once I learned this, I signed up to be a book reviewer for her company. She was very happy with the work I did, and she knew I was looking for other work, so she soon hired me to interview authors and write press releases. This was not enough money by any means to leave my day job, but it allowed me to earn money on the side, become more familiar with the publishing industry, and use my writing skills. Victor and Irene also asked me to be the guest host for the *Authors Access* show whenever one of them was out, which I quickly agreed to. In time,

Victor, who owned Loving Healing Press and Modern History Press, also agreed to publish my books *King Arthur's Children* and *The Gothic Wanderer*. The three of us also produced the book, *Authors Access: Thirty Success Secrets for Authors and Publishers*, which featured articles by many of the show's guests on topics they had been interviewed about. I would also write several articles for the book.

That same month, when I was first interviewed on *Authors Access*, the Upper Peninsula Publishers and Authors Association held its annual conference and hosted Patrick Snow, a bestselling author and publishing coach, as its keynote speaker. To save the organization money, Patrick agreed to stay in someone's home, and since I had a spare room, I agreed to host him. This simple act of saying yes was one of the best things I ever did. I knew if Patrick stayed with me, I'd have the opportunity to pick his brain about the publishing industry. What I didn't expect was that he would be impressed that I had a PhD, and that as a publishing coach, he was looking for editors for his clients' books. I immediately agreed to edit books for Patrick's clients, and within about a year, I was getting enough referrals from Patrick and enough work from Reader Views to keep me busy every night after work.

Once Patrick asked me to edit for his clients, I felt I had better make sure my editing and proofreading skills were up to snuff. That might seem silly since I had a doctorate and had taught English, but I was conscientious, and I knew publishing industry standards were not necessarily those of academia. As a result, I responded to an ad for a proofreader at the *Marquette Monthly*, a local monthly magazine. The job was fifteen to twenty hours a month, so it would not be too time-consuming and it would allow me to hone my skills. It turned out those hours all had to be put in the week before the magazine's deadline, so once hired, I regularly had a very busy last week of the month.

As you can imagine, between working a full-time job, doing work on the side for Reader Views and *Marquette Monthly*, and editing books for Patrick's clients, every minute of nearly every day was full, and I was starting to feel very stressed. However, one thing that helped my stress a lot was that since 2006, just before my first book came out, I had started attending a local group focused on the Law of Attraction and particularly the Teachings of Abraham. Abraham is a collection of entities channeled through Esther Hicks that answers people's questions about the universe, the meaning of life, and how to make the Law of Attraction work in their lives. I felt like the Law of Attraction was definitely working in my life since I was now attracting what I wanted— book sales and meaningful work. By this point, I had published four books and I had a sizeable amount of extra income coming in—the equivalent of half my day job income.

My day job was very demanding and stressful, though, and I could barely keep up with everything there. One day at work, I had a meeting with my boss and the two supervisors who worked under me to see how we could better distribute the work, since they all knew I had too much on my plate. Beforehand, I was asked to make a list of all my tasks and responsibilities, and then we would see what could be moved off my list. When that meeting was over, one item had been moved off my list and two had been added. Obviously, the meeting had not worked to my benefit.

A few days later at my Abraham-Hicks group, we watched a video in which someone asked Abraham how to handle feeling overwhelmed at work. Abraham said to make a list and then rip it in half. Next, tell your boss which half you are going to do. Well, I'd already made my list and it hadn't worked out for me, but I spent several days thinking about Abraham's advice. Then I realized that my work didn't include just my day job, but all my side jobs. If I were to rip my to-do list in half, it meant I would either have to quit doing all the work on the side or quit my day job. Guess which one I picked.

I felt so elated and relieved when I realized I was going to quit my day job. Of course, I was nervous about it, and I wanted to be cautious about how I did it. I knew it would be hard to replace me at my day job and that time would be needed to train my successor, so I gave my notice the first week of December and agreed to stay until Friday, January 30, 2009. That would give me some extra income over the holidays and time to save some money. I also had several weeks of vacation time saved up that would help tide me over in case I didn't have enough editing work in the beginning. But without my day job, I would also have more time to focus on finding editing work.

It was a scary leap of faith, but I took it regardless. The first couple of months of self-employment, I worried how I would make my mortgage payments, but by spring, I had constant work that has not let up since.

So that's the story of how I became a freelance editor. It happened in a roundabout way, but everything I learned in the jobs I had and my determination to continue writing ultimately got me where I was meant to be. What happened since—how I've maintained an editing business and learned to find balance between my work and personal life—will be described in the following chapters.

When I tell people what I do, they often say, "Oh, you have the dream job. You get to work from home." I'll tell you right now that being an editor is not a dream job. It is probably the best job for me, personally, but it is not cushy or stress-free. People say to me, "Oh, you can be flexible with your time," and my friends think I'm always free for lunch, but I always work more than forty hours a week, and often more than fifty. My relatives seem to think all I do is sit at home and write my own books, and therefore, I'm free to go run errands for them. The truth is, working for yourself from home means you have to fight to keep your boundaries strong. Yes, if I really want to take time to do something non-work related during the week, I can, but I also may have to make up for it by working an evening or a weekend. And yes, working for yourself means you can be a nomad. You can travel wherever you want and still do your work—but if you are self-employed and have no one to help you, that means checking emails and replying to clients on your vacations, or finding someone you trust to keep your business afloat while you're away. If you want to live abroad, of course, you will take your work with you. I just want to be very clear from the start that being a nomad editor doesn't mean just sunbathing on the Riviera; it means working hard so you can afford to take the time to sunbathe wherever and whenever you want.

If you have the skills and the right attitude, I'm sure you will enjoy working from home and doing the work, but just as with any job, editing has its frustrations and difficulties. You certainly can't just work a few hours a day and then play the rest of the time if you want to support yourself. Books take a long time to edit, and most authors are in a hurry to get their books published. I easily spend anywhere from twenty to forty or more hours on every book I edit. With some books, it's been 100 hours. A book can be several weeks of work because between client phone calls and emails and other interruptions, I can usually only get about five hours of actual editing done in a day, and I always work eight and often nine or ten hours a day. Of course, I eat lunch and breakfast in that time, but usually while reading and responding to emails.

As a freelance editor, it's best to commit to working regular hours or a certain number of hours and not being easily swayed from them. The advantage is that most of your friends will have day jobs and be busy working too, but retired friends and relatives will want your time. Yes, if you want to go for a walk or drive to the grocery store during your work hours, you can do that, but I recommend you commit to a regular schedule as much as possible. I'll talk more about all of this and the daily frustrations and triumphs of being an editor in the remainder of this book. But realize right now that this job is work just like any other job; it just gives you more flexibility so you can also be a nomad.

Best of all, you get to spend your day playing with words. Sometimes those words won't make much sense because your client can barely write a complete sentence, but other times, you get hired to edit a really fabulous book. Most of the time, you are editing a mediocre book that you are helping to turn into a good book. You also get to meet some fascinating people because, let's face it, while a lot of bad books are written, it takes someone with a lot of gumption and motivation to write a book, and most people who write books do have something interesting or original to say, maybe even something fascinating or innovative, even if they need you to ensure they say it well.

At the end of the day, I feel the best thing about my job is that I am helping to bring books into the world that will make a difference for who knows how many people. Whether those books are entertaining novels that help people forget their troubles, business books that help people become financially independent, or self-help books that help people overcome drug addictions or dysfunctional behaviors, books help people. Consequently, while I'm in the editing business, I'm also in the people-helping business, and that's a wonderful thing!

Being an editor is not always easy, but it's still wonderful. In the chapters that follow, I'll share the pros and cons of being a freelance editor. I'll teach you what to expect, and I'll offer resources for acquiring the skills you need to succeed. Ultimately, by learning from the mistakes I've made and the successes I've had, you'll be better prepared to have a long and enjoyable career as an editor.

Chapter 2
Grammar, Punctuation, Compassion, and Perspiration:
An Editor's Skills

"When you look at people who are successful, you will find that they aren't the people who are motivated, but have consistency in their motivation."

— Arsene Wenger, French Football Coach and Player

IF YOU WANT to be a freelance editor, you will need to be very knowledgeable about the English language and have strong writing skills. But you will also need other skills, such as a sense of style, an ability to retain and imitate an author's tone, excellent attention to detail, self-motivation, time-management skills, good customer service skills, and accounting skills. Let's look at the basics of each of these and how you can acquire them.

Knowledge of the English Language and Style Manuals

First and foremost, to be an editor, you need to have a strong grasp of the English language. You will discover as you edit books that there is so much about the English language that you do not know and that you will learn, but make sure you are as knowledgeable as possible before you begin. This means you should know the difference between who and whom, affect and effect, a colon and a semicolon, and whether to italicize, bold, place in quotation marks, or do nothing at all to emphasize a song, book title, or company name, and, of course, that's only the beginning.

You will also need to be knowledgeable about the proper style manual for the type of book you are editing. Here are the basic style manuals to familiarize yourself with:

- **The Chicago Manual of Style (CMOS):** Almost every publisher uses *The Chicago Manual of Style*, but there are exceptions. If you are working for a publisher, ask which manual it uses and then acquire a copy. *The Chicago Manual of Style* is available online. I would recommend getting an online subscription to it so you always have the most recent information at your fingertips, since the manual does change its opinions on various issues with each new edition. One of the key differences between *The Chicago Manual of Style* and the Associated Press (AP) style is that it prefers the serial comma. Recent changes that *The Chicago Manual of Style* have made include promoting post office protocol in not using periods in abbreviations. For example, US President Barack Obama would not include periods in US. It also prefers that all numbers under 100 be written out, while other style manuals may prefer only numbers under ten or twenty be written out. By subscribing online, you have easy access to the answer you are seeking. You may also want to order a paper copy of the manual, but honestly, it is not easy to find answers in the paper manuals, so being able to search online is your best option. You can access *The Chicago Manual of Style* online at www.chicagomanualofstyle.org. Remember that you can write off your purchase or yearly subscription to the website version as a business expense. Anything you buy for your business is a business expense and must be documented. (We'll discuss keeping track of business expenses in Chapter 4.)

- **Turabian:** This style is basically the same as *CMOS* but for students. It's often required as the style for dissertations in many disciplines, including business, history, religious studies, and the fine arts. The stylebook for it is *A Manual for Writers of Research Papers, Theses, and Dissertations: Chicago Manual of Style for Students and Researchers.* It is currently in its ninth edition.

- **Associated Press (AP) style:** If you will be editing for magazines or newspapers, you will want to brush up on AP style by getting a copy of *The Associated Press Stylebook*. There are some serious differences between AP and *CMOS* styles. Besides not using serial commas, AP only uses single rather than double quotations in headlines. Many of AP's style decisions result from a desire to save space in newsprint so there is no place for extra commas or extra quotation marks. I recommend you get a job working at a newspaper or magazine to familiarize yourself with AP style if you think that is the kind of editing you would like to do.

- **American Psychological Association (APA) style:** APA is similar to *CMOS*, but it has some noted differences. It tends to be used for medical and psychological works and also by the sciences more than other style manuals. Again, ask your clients which style manual they need to use. Most self-published or beginning authors won't know, so then I would default to *CMOS*, but if you end up editing dissertations for students, you will have to find out which style guide is required and adapt to those guidelines. Either way, get yourself a copy of the *Publication Copy of the American Psychological Association.* I have a Kindle version because it is easy to search in it for what I need.

- **Modern Language Association (MLA Style):** Few books to my knowledge use MLA style, but again, if you end up editing dissertations, this is a style you may need to use, especially if you are editing works that fall within the category of the arts. If you were an English major, MLA style is probably what you were trained to use. One of the big differences of this style guide is its use of parenthetical documentation (also called in-text or in-line citations) instead of footnotes.

- **Christian Writers Style Manual:** If you are editing anything of a religious nature, you will definitely want to get a copy of this manual. You will be surprised by some of its preferences. You will likely have authors submit manuscripts to you in which all pronouns referencing God will be capitalized, but this manual recommends that you not capitalize them. After all, they are not capitalized in the Bible. In fact, the capitalization of pronouns referencing God is a Victorian convention that many writers still retain. As with any style manual guidelines, it is best to point out to authors what the style manual says and then let them decide whether they want to abide by it or not. I've edited several books where authors have insisted on capitalizing the God/Jesus pronouns, in which case, I go ahead and make sure they stay capitalized and are consistent—after all, the customer is always right—but I always feel it is my job to let clients know when something is not consistent with the rules of a style manual. They can choose to do otherwise, but then I have my bases covered if later anyone tells the author something is wrong.

- **AMA Manual of Style:** This manual, published by the American Medical Association, is generally used for anyone doing medical or scientific writing.

Note that various disciplines may have their own guidelines. For example, there is no style manual for engineering, but it does have rules about citations. It is always best to check with authors on any style guidelines in their disciplines and request copies if there are specific guidelines for journals they are submitting to if there is no style manual for you to purchase.

Style manuals also differ by country. If you end up editing for people in Canada, Great Britain, Australia, or New Zealand, you will need to know the conventions of British English as opposed to American English; some of those differences are in spelling, others are in punctuation. Always ask the author or publisher you are working with whether the book's primary audience will be in the United States or in another English-speaking country and then follow the rules as appropriate. You can find a list of standard style manuals for other countries at Wikipedia by searching "list of style guides."

Before you branch out on your own, also make sure you get some experience editing by working for someone else. Working for a newspaper or magazine is an excellent way to gain such experience. You can also work for a publisher. Other ways to gain experience are through technical writing in corporate America, or teaching English and writing and grading student papers.

Likely, you already have the writing and editing skills needed from your past fields of study, but you may need to acquire or brush up your skills in other areas.

I also recommend that once you begin editing books, you create your own style manual for any oddities not covered in the style manual you usually use or just issues that arise that you don't want to keep looking up every time. An additional advantage to creating your own style guide is that if you eventually find someone to help you with editing, a document exists that everyone can refer to. The following are a few items from my style manual as an example of what you might create. Listings are alphabetical.

Superior Book Productions Style Guide

Overall, use the *Chicago Manual of Style (CMOS)*. However, a few exceptions have been made below so be sure to familiarize yourself with this style guide. If you have a question that you can't find the answer to here or in *CMOS*, ask Tyler what is preferred and he will add the item to the list or open it up for discussion.

Abbreviations/Acronyms—Always write out the full term upon first use followed by the abbreviation (except very well-known abbreviations such as FBI. For example, "At Superior Book Productions (SBP), we use the *Chicago Manual of Style (CMOS)*." Per the *CMOS*, periods are no longer needed in abbreviations, including US, DC, and PhD. However, note that US is only to be abbreviated as an adjective. For example, US President Barack Obama.

Ages—Always written out, in accordance with number rule below.

a.k.a.—Use the periods and lowercase per *CMOS*.

As—When "as" is used to mean "because" or "since" it should be changed to "because" or "since" to avoid confusion with its other time-related meaning.

All right—Always two words, never one.

A while—Always two words, never one, including in the phrase "once in a while."

Bachelor's degree—Not a proper noun. Degree titles should be lowercase unless the nouns involved are proper nouns (bachelor's degree in illustration, bachelor's degree in English).

Backseat—One word.

Childcare—One word.

Cleanup—One word when used as a noun; two words when used as a verb phrase. The same is true with breakup, pickup, and setup.

Capitalization—For titles, any word of four or more letters should be capitalized, regardless of its part of speech. Short pronouns or verbs, such as "is" and "it" should also be capitalized. All caps should always be avoided in the main text because it is considered shouting at the reader. Use italics instead for emphasis.

Commas—Always use the serial comma.

Dates—As a general rule, always write out the full date: January 18, not Jan. 18, exceptions being charts and graphs where space is an issue.

Daycare—One word, no hyphen.

A Sense of Style and When to Break the Rules

Most authors I work with are thrilled with the work I do for them. They always tell me I make them sound good. That said, as an editor, it can be tempting to rewrite someone's entire book so it reads better. Restrain yourself. Yes, sometimes it is necessary to rewrite almost every sentence, especially if the client is not a native speaker of English. However, you need to remember the book is the author's book and not yours. I always make it clear to clients that I want to enhance their voices to create the best possible versions of those voices. However, everyone has little pet phrases or wording preferences, and as long as they are not grammatically incorrect, even if they are words I would not use myself, I will usually leave them alone to retain the author's style.

In *The Subversive Copy Editor*, Carrol Saller advises that editors take guidance from the medical profession by making it also our motto to "First, do no harm." This motto is especially true when it comes to retaining the author's voice. I always do a free edit sample when I come up with a quote for an author (more about edit samples in Chapter 3). Edit samples allow authors to see the kinds of changes I would make and ensure they are comfortable with them. For example, authors may not want me to write out numbers, even though it's what *The Chicago Manual of Style* says to do. Authors may have grammatically incorrect catch phrases they have used for years printed in all their marketing materials that they may not want to change. (For example, Apple's "Think Different" should technically be "Think Differently," but Steve Jobs decided he wanted "different" to be used as a noun so it would be more effective to get the message across.) Such decisions are ultimately the author's and so I abide by them.

The author is the boss, but you are the expert. It is up to you to know the rules, and sometimes the perception of rules, and recommend the best course. For example, in the past, I always rewrote split infinitives (when the infinitive of a verb, such as "to jump" is split by inserting an adverb in the middle of it, such as "to quickly jump.") However, many grammarians argue that split infinitives are not a true error, so I've come to accept that some of them, if rewritten, will just result in a sentence being more awkward than if the split infinitive is allowed to remain. Consider how the original *Star Trek* series introduced the phrase "to boldly go where no man has gone before." While "to boldly go" is a split infinitive, to rewrite it as "to go boldly" or worse, "boldly to go," just doesn't have the same ring to it, so I would leave it alone. However, today, while I might leave "to boldly go" alone, I would change "no man" to "no one" to be more inclusive. In fact, when *Star Trek: The Next Generation* aired in 1987, the phrase was changed to "no one."

Another issue that has come to the forefront recently is subject-pronoun agreement. Words such as anyone, everyone, and nobody have, since the mid-eighteenth century, been considered singular; however, this was not the case prior, and it is not the case today. Almost every author I work with will write a sentence like, "Everyone should know how to tie their shoes." In the recent past, the correct version would have been "Everyone should know how to tie his shoes" but male pronouns standing in for all humans is giving way to more inclusive language. That said, "Everyone should know how to tie his or her shoes" sounds wordy and awkward. "Her or his shoes," since we are unaccustomed to putting the female pronoun first, sounds even more awkward—an awkwardness we will need to get over if we don't revert to "their." To solve these problems, I'd be tempted to rewrite the sentence as, "All people should know how to tie their shoes," so the subject is plural and matches the pronoun. I can't say I think that sounds great, but as a general rule, I aim always to make subjects plural in these cases; however, in some cases this is not possible, so then I default to using "his or her." None of these are satisfactory solutions so you'll have to decide for yourself what fits best with the style of the book you're editing and also what the author prefers. Ultimately, I might just leave this sentence as "Everyone should know how to tie their shoes." Honestly, it's the best-sounding option. Furthermore, some authors want to use "their" to cover both sexes regardless of subject-pronoun agreement. A solid argument exists for this usage since it has historical precedence, is similar to plural or singular "you," covers both sexes, and also shows respect for transgender people who may not want to be identified with a single gender. Both Dictionary.com and Webster's Dictionary now accept "they" as a singular pronoun, as does the Oxford English Dictionary. Who am I to argue with them?

These and similar issues should be discussed with authors upfront so they can make the best decisions for their books. You need to remember that customers are always right, even when they are not, and abide by their decisions since they are paying you, or alternatively, turn down their business because you feel it goes against your principles. I have very rarely been asked to do something I was unwilling to do (there's a story where I did say no in Chapter 3), so it's usually not an issue; plus, the vast majority of authors I've worked with have simply been willing to let me make the decisions, trusting to my expertise once I explain the reason for a change.

Finally, a word about formal versus informal English. When we speak, we are generally informal. However, no one wants to read a book that's written like how we speak, especially not complete with hems and haws, sentence fragments, and repeated words—read a transcript of an oral interview sometime and you'll see what I mean. Books are formal writing so they should follow the rules of formal writing, but again, the author's tone also needs to be retained. Here's an example: In academia, use of contractions is frowned upon—they are viewed as slang. However, while this book you're reading is a formal piece of writing, I want to convey a reader-friendly tone as if we are having a conversation. Therefore, I have no problem using contractions where I think they sound more natural and make sentences flow better. If this were a doctoral dissertation, I would be less inclined to use contractions. That said, I can't tell you how many novels I've edited where authors have not used any contractions in the dialogue. As a result, the characters sound stilted and unrealistic. I will add a healthy dose of contractions wherever needed. Again, the degree of formality used all depends on the book, its purpose, and the message and tone the author wants to convey. These are all matters that you, as the editor, need to be aware of so you can make the best decisions or help your clients make them.

Consistency and Attention to Detail

Your grammar skills don't matter much if you're not able to spot a misspelled word or an inconsistent use of commas. In my opinion, attention to detail is an editor's most important skill. You will be amazed by the errors you catch after a manuscript has been "edited" by the author. Be understanding; authors likely have bigger concerns than remembering that the publishing industry only uses one space after a period or exclamation mark, etc., so don't be surprised if they always use two or don't know when to use a hyphen or a dash. These are all things you will need to fix for them and they are relying on you to get right.

I always turn on the track changes feature in Microsoft Word (MS Word) for clients so when they send me back their manuscripts, I can see everything they've changed in a different color; then I can look very carefully at the changes and fix any new errors authors have introduced such as extra spaces after periods. (Sometimes, an author manages to turn off the track changes feature and returns the manuscript without me being able to see the changes. If this happens, you can compare the new document with the earlier version by using the "compare" feature in MS Word, found under the Review tab.)

Because authors insert all kinds of extra spaces in their documents, I also always have the "invisible" characters turned on when I edit. The invisible characters will show you a little dot where every space between words exists, as well as all the paragraph returns, tabs, or any other formatting characters. In short, being an editor also means being a manuscript formatter. There are quick and easy ways to do a search and replace for extra spaces, to get rid of tabs, and to fix a multitude of other spacing and formatting errors clients will make.

You will likely have many clients who are not very computer literate. I've received manuscripts where the client hit return twice at the end of every line, thinking that was how to double-space a manuscript. This person learned to type on a typewriter and never learned how to use a word-processing program properly. You will need to learn how to fix all these issues quickly using search and replace features; otherwise, the manuscript will go to the layout person and all those spaces will cause problems and result in extra lines running onto pages where they aren't needed or other weird spacing issues. Hopefully, the layout person will catch and fix these problems, but not every layout person is created the same, so the better you are at catching such issues in the manuscript, the smoother the layout will go for you and the author. A good editor will submit the cleanest manuscript possible to the layout person to make the layout go as smoothly as possible. One of the first books I edited resulted in the layout person telling me I had submitted the cleanest manuscript she had ever seen, and as a result, she was always going to recommend me to authors she worked with. Keeping the layout person happy should be your second priority, only after keeping the author happy.

Another major detail to pay attention to is spelling and how specific names or phrases are used. For example, if the client is writing a business book and keeps referring to XYZ, Inc., you want to make sure it is not XYZ Inc on another page, or XYZ Incorporated, or just XYZ in other places. I always do searches for terms and names that repeat throughout the book to ensure they are consistent. It is often a good idea to keep a style sheet for the book, listing such details so the client will know what you fixed and what certain items should look like going forward. You might even find that the client wants it to be xyz, inc., so providing a style sheet for the client to review is always a good idea. This also helps the author identify inconsistencies and verify which styles/word forms should be used. You can then do a search and replace of terms to adhere to the author's preference.

I could go on and on about the importance of consistency and attention to detail. The bottom line is to check and question everything. If you're not sure about the spelling of a word, look it up. I can't tell you how many times I have seen a word spelled three ways in a book about meditation (also misspelled mediation and meditaton). It is your job to make sure meditation is spelled correctly everywhere. More common errors might be something like the use of both dialog and dialogue in the same book. Unless computer software is being discussed, dialogue should be used. Paying attention to these details can become tedious, especially if you don't know the words being used yourself. I once edited a book set in Thailand in which the author had nearly every geographic location misspelled. In addition, foreign locations might have multiple spellings in English. You need to figure out which spelling appears to be the most common or accepted and be consistent with it throughout the book. It can be a lot of work to look up all those terms or place names, but that's what you are being paid to do; you can never expect your clients to be consistent or pay attention to details; now and then, one will, but most won't bother because that is why they hired you.

Self-Motivation and Time Management

You can have all of the editing skills and grammar expertise in the world, but none of that is going to help if you are not self-motivated. Good writers know sitting around waiting for inspiration will get you nowhere. Writing requires hard work and dedication, and so does editing. You need to be prepared to work long hours alone. Fortunately, like many writers, we editors tend to be introverts who enjoy our own company. We are our own best friends, and we also have to be our own bosses—and who better to have for a boss than yourself? But sometimes you do have to be the kind of boss who cracks the whip—you can be the soothing best friend to yourself later.

I will not try to share my self-motivation secrets. After half a lifetime of trying to motivate people and understand why they don't do things the way I would, I have given up. The truth is, you cannot make people do something they don't want to do. People are either motivated or they're not. As a freelance editor, you need to be motivated; you have to want to be your own boss, you have to want to do a stellar job for your clients, and you have to want to play wordsmith all day.

That said, even if you are self-motivated, you also need basic time-management and organizational skills so you know how to prioritize your work.

For me, good time-management requires doing three things:

1. Having a schedule. No matter how rigid your schedule is, the phone, email, the Schwan's delivery person, etc. are all going to conspire to destroy your schedule. Regardless, make a schedule for each day and try to stick to it. It doesn't have to be as rigid as "answer email from 8-9 a.m." but you can make a list on paper or in your head of what you need to do that day and work down the list as the day goes on.

2. Begin each day with your biggest task and work toward the smallest. Determine the most important, immediate, or time-consuming tasks for that day. Do them in the order of largest to smallest, and do not let anything stop you from accomplishing them. You'll soon find, if you're successful, that you have work lined up for days in advance. I don't always schedule things, but I generally know what I'll do for the next few days and then can switch things around as needed. Here is what a typical couple of weeks of work will look like for me:

Monday: Proofread David's book and send for layout.

Tuesday: Edit the revisions for Shirley's book and send it back to her. Get started editing Joe's book.

Wednesday: Edit Joe's book.

Thursday: Edit Joe's book.

Friday: Write up notes for Joe to make revisions and return book to him. Get started editing Alex's book.

Saturday: Respond to emails.

Sunday: Respond to emails, including to Shirley who sent the next revisions of her book, and Michelle who sent you her new book.

Monday: Do an edit sample for Michelle. Review Shirley's final corrections and send final manuscript to layout person. Continue editing Alex's book.

Tuesday: Finish editing Alex's book and return to him with revision suggestions.

Wednesday: Start editing Michelle's book.

Thursday: Edit Michelle's book.

Friday: Edit Michelle's book.

Saturday: Respond to emails, including to Joe to let him know you got his revisions.

Sunday: Respond to emails, including Alex's questions about revisions he should consider.

Monday: Finish editing Michelle's book and return it to her. Review layout proofs of Shirley's book. Begin second edit of Joe's book.

Tuesday: Review layout proofs of David's book. Work on second edit of Joe's book.

You get the idea. If all goes well, you will be working on three to six books at a time, sending them back and forth to the authors. As a result, you constantly need to keep the ball rolling. Of course, while I might block out the entire day to work on Michelle's book, that doesn't mean I don't do other things. Clients are emailing me all day wanting me to add a sentence to their About the Author pages, layout is sending me PDFs of book covers to proofread, and other clients are asking me questions about how to get an ISBN number, but the bulk of my day—five or six hours anyway—is being devoted to Michelle's book, which will likely take me three or four days to do the first edit, depending on how long it is and how good of a writer Michelle is.

You'll also note in the schedule that I included Saturday and Sunday. This leads me to point three:

3. Manage Your Email and Don't Let It Manage You. Trust me, I've read (and edited) countless books that talk about how to manage your email. They're all great in a perfect world, but I haven't found one yet that works. Authors can be very demanding. Their books are like their children, so they want your constant attention. Some of my clients think nothing of calling me at 9 p.m. on Friday or 10 a.m. on Sunday. Depending on the client, why I think the person is calling, and what I'm doing, I may or may not answer (provided I know from Caller ID who it is). I've heard that you need to train your clients on what to expect from you in terms of a response, but to train them, you have to begin training them from the start; however, if you start your relationship by waiting two days to answer an email, just because the person sent it on Friday evening, and the person is shopping that evening for an editor and another editor responds within the hour, you're likely to lose that job, even if you're a better editor. (We'll talk more about this topic and how to set boundaries with clients in Chapter 9.)

For this reason, I've remained very responsive to my clients and prospective clients. Most of them are surprised that I almost always answer the phone. If I don't, I will usually call them back quickly. If they call during regular business hours, I guarantee I will answer unless I truly cannot. If they call during the weekend, I might call them back later or Monday. Most of my clients, however, will email me. I recommend telling your clients that email is the best way to communicate with you. An email will always take less of your time than a phone call. You will also have the email to refer back to if you have questions or can't remember something. Plus, you can answer an email at your convenience; you can still be responsive with email, but you don't have to drop everything like you do when you answer the phone. Furthermore, if you want to be a nomad editor, you may not always have the best cellphone reception, so be sure your outgoing voicemail message includes your email address and when clients can expect you to return a call. It is also helpful to tell people your time zone so they will call at reasonable times.

Don't let your clients abuse your time, whether by phone or email. For example, if on Saturday morning a client sends you an email saying, "Do you have time for a quick call?" or "a five-minute call," I would just say no. If what they want can't be said in an email, then it won't be a quick call. You need to learn to say no and protect your personal time while at the same time being responsive. Tell your client, "No, I have other plans today and I am busy tomorrow, but I'm free anytime you want to talk next week." Granted, your plans for the weekend may be to take a long soak in the tub or go for a bike ride, but you have to keep your appointments with yourself as well as with your clients if you want to maintain work-life balance and your sanity.

I do try to be responsive by checking email and responding on Saturday and Sunday mornings. Email is part of my regular schedule because I like getting it out of the way. During the weekend, I usually spend less than an hour responding to email and then the rest of my day is free. You may even want to go so far as to spend this time writing your responses and saving them as drafts to send on Monday (depending on the client's needs). Do not respond to clients on Saturday morning within two minutes of receiving an email or they'll think you are free to talk. Send an email in the afternoon instead. I admit, I check my email two or three times a day on the weekend, but this usually only takes me a few minutes each time. Yes, I am a workaholic, hopefully a recovering one, so I try very hard to manage my time, but I also try to manage my stress by not having fifty emails to answer Monday morning, which would keep me from getting much editing done. I know other editors who have no problem working nights or weekends, and that's fine for them—being able to be flexible is, after all, a major reason I'm self-employed—but as a recovering workaholic, I try to keep a schedule and only check my email every few hours, just so I don't feel overwhelmed trying to answer it all on Monday morning.

When I started out in this business, I worked 8 a.m. to 6 p.m. Monday through Friday and usually worked six or so hours on Saturday and maybe four on Sunday. I remember only taking Easter and Christmas off my first year as a full-time editor, but eventually, I learned how to set boundaries to preserve my sanity. Today, I typically work 8:30 a.m. to 5:00 p.m. Monday through Friday. I will keep an eye on my email from 5 to 8 p.m., but I will not do any editing work during that time. On the weekend, I spend no more than an hour each day responding to clients. That results in about a forty-seven- to fifty-hour work week (as opposed to my old sixty-plus-hour work week) and that's enough for anyone. (I'm also an author, so I typically spend an hour each evening writing my own books and two or three hours on both Saturday and Sunday writing, which still counts as work and results in about a sixty-hour work week regardless.)

Accept right now that if you're self-employed and successful, you'll have to work some extra hours, but remember, you're working from home, or Paris, or Tokyo, or wherever you want, and working for yourself. Think of all the time you're not wasting commuting and use that time to keep your clients happy.

Also, be understanding. Your clients likely have day jobs of their own, so they may only be able to ask you questions or send you emails on the weekend or in the evening. Be compassionate and understanding of their time and schedules as well as your own.

Now, because you have a 50,000-word book to edit in the next three days—and you have to get it done in that time frame because you have two more waiting, not to mention four books you have sent back to authors for revisions that could come back at any moment—when are you going to find time to answer all your email? Here is what I've found works for me.

The last thing I want to do when I first get out of bed is to start responding to email. I find it overwhelming, and I would first like a little quiet time in the morning. So, instead, I get up, get dressed, make my coffee or tea, and then sit down and edit for an hour or two. I usually start around 8:30 a.m. Then about 10 a.m. I make breakfast and check my email while I eat. I've found that 10 a.m. is the perfect time to check email because, since I'm in the Eastern time zone, clients who emailed me overnight will get replies around 7:00 or 7:30 a.m. if they're on the Pacific Coast, likely before they start work, and before they even wake up if they're in Hawaii or Alaska. Even people on the East Coast aren't likely to start emailing me until 7 or 8 a.m., so I'm still getting back to them within a few hours.

About 10:30 or 11 a.m., when I've responded to everyone, I close down my email and go back to editing. For the rest of the day, I will edit for an hour, then read my email, then edit for an hour, then read my email. I do this so I can get a full hour of work done at a time, and I can still respond to clients within an hour or so.

I guarantee that if you leave your email open while trying to edit, every time your computer dings or you see the email icon appear out of the corner of your eye, your brain will start wondering what that email could be about and you won't be concentrating on your client's book; that's a time-waster, so close the email. You may find that you prefer to wait two hours between email checks, and that's fine, but after every hour, I tend to get up and refill my water glass, go to the bathroom, or just stretch my legs, so I also find it's a good time to check my email. If I wait two hours to get up, my legs and butt start to get stiff. Also, you do not want a client to wait too long for a reply. While you may not think two hours is too long to wait, clients may not agree; some will be impatient enough to pick up the phone and call if you don't reply quickly, and I want to avoid as many phone calls as possible because they are much longer interruptions than emails, especially since I pride myself on always being responsive, in part by answering my phone. After all, my clients are my business and not an interruption really (just an interruption of my editing).

Another reason I check my email every hour is because it is easy to remember to record one hour of work in my spreadsheet to keep track of my time. We'll talk more about tracking your hours per project in Chapter 3; for now, just know that you need to track your hours if you want to get paid accurately. Even if you're not being paid hourly, but by a flat rate for the project, you need to track your time to ensure you are bidding properly and not overcharging—or, more likely, undercharging—for your time.

Patience and Compassion

The final skill you need to master as a freelance editor is patience. Of course, you need patience in any job dealing with the public, but you need a lot as an editor because authors will repeatedly ask you what you may think are elementary questions. I am sure when I go to the garage to get my car fixed I sound clueless to the mechanic because I know almost nothing about cars. Similarly, your clients might sound completely clueless to you—after all, you might wonder how anyone writing a book cannot know how to use commas, or not know the difference between a foreword (most will call it a "forward") and an introduction, or not know how to double-space a manuscript, or even how to send an attachment via email. Believe me, a lot of authors don't know these things.

Just remember that not everyone is a writer or reader, but everyone has a story or information to share with the world, and you have a job because these people need your help to make that sharing possible. If you are an author yourself, you know publishing your first book comes with a big learning curve, so be patient with your clients and give them the care you would want to receive if you were in their shoes.

A lot of the authors I work with are senior citizens. They've worked hard all their lives and have been busy raising their families, but now they finally have time to write their books. However, sometimes they're a little forgetful. Sometimes they don't have the best computer skills. Be as patient as possible with them. You might have to talk to them on the phone to walk them through how to attach the manuscript via email. You might have to wade through twenty emails without attachments. Since you can't see the client's computer, this can be frustrating. Try to be helpful and patient, but to save yourself time and frustration, you can also suggest the author ask a computer-savvy family member or friend for help.

Also, remember that not everyone's strengths are your strengths. That's why these authors will pay you. I've edited books for incredibly intelligent people: entrepreneurs with million-dollar businesses, lawyers, doctors, and ministers. They have had more important (for them) things to worry about than how to perfect their writing. That's why they are paying you. Just as the garage mechanic might not know the difference between a hyphen and an em dash, so I am not able to change the oil in my car. But both the garage mechanic and I can learn if we really want to. You may be tempted to try to teach the garage mechanic-turned-author how to write complete sentences. However, I've found, with rare exception, most authors don't want to learn how to write better. They just want their books edited and published.

Fiction writers tend to be an exception, but not always. Despite many authors being unwilling to learn, I do always put comments in the margins explaining why I make certain changes. I do that mostly so they won't change it back when they make their revisions. Occasionally, an author takes my comments to heart and the writing improves, but this is rare. In fact, one time I suggested to a repeat client that she might write better if she took a creative writing class. She said she didn't need to because she had me. Well, truthfully, I did help improve her writing on a sentence structure level, but I wasn't a miracle worker, and she would never take my advice on changes to the plot. Still, understand that your clients often have other priorities, like launching a new product, visiting sick parishioners, or winning a professional basketball game, so it's up to you to ensure their sentences have appropriate punctuation and correct spelling. If you do help improve an author's writing skills, treasure those moments, but don't expect them.

Patience and compassion—don't forget to keep them in your back pocket at all times.

Summary

Don't even think about trying to make money as an editor if you don't have the skills I've shared in this chapter. It won't happen because you'll burn out quickly or you'll be doing second-rate work that clients will soon catch on to. However, if you have these skills, or believe you can develop them, you're ready to start thinking about how to begin building your business, which will be the focus of the next few chapters.

Chapter 3
Is This Worth My Time?:
What to Charge

"Don't sell yourself short. No one will value you. Set a fair price for you, your book, your services, whatever it is that you have to offer. Most of us set way too low a price. Put it a little higher than you would normally be inclined to do."

— John Kremer, *1001 Ways to Market Your Books*

FIGURING OUT HOW much to charge is one of the most difficult and most important tasks for any entrepreneur, and for an editor, it's harder than it is for most. It's not like selling hot dogs where you set one price for your hot dogs and every person pays the same. It's not that simple because every book you edit will be different. Some will be 25,000 words long and some might be 250,000. Some will be written by PhDs in creative writing. Some will be written by people for whom English is their second language. Some will be written by native speakers of English who couldn't write a complete sentence to save their lives. Some will be written by high school dropouts who can write better than most graduate students. Every book is different, and as a result, the price for editing each book will be different.

Before we go further, let me caution you: *Never, ever, ever—I repeat—never, ever, ever agree to edit a book or agree to a price for a book you have not yet seen.* I learned this lesson the hard way. The first author I ever proofread a book for called me up, told me how long (or rather short) his book was, and asked me if I could do the job for $300. I accepted. I should have asked for $600. I lost a lot of time and money on that book because I didn't look at the quality of the writing before setting the price. I learned from that experience that I need to evaluate and provide a customized price quote for every book.

Like many people starting their own businesses, I had a hard time asking for what I was worth, or even knowing what that was. I thought if I made as much as I had made at my day job, that was all that mattered, and so I charged accordingly. Don't fall into this kind of thinking. For one thing, at your day job you probably had benefits, including health insurance. As a freelance editor, you have to pay for all those benefits out of your own pocket, so you need to charge more to cover them. Furthermore, even though I track how many hours I work on a book, even if I assume a book will be a forty-hour project, I have to make allowance for all the emails and phone calls I'll have with the author. With this in mind, I add a little time to the quotes to cover administrative tasks, client contact, and unforeseen circumstances.

Setting an Hourly Wage

You can begin to figure out what you should charge per hour by doing some industry research. A simple online search for "How much do freelance editors make per hour?" will give you lots of good information. As a base, at the time of this book's publication, most editors make between $25 and $75 an hour.

Start out at a price you feel comfortable with and you think your clientele will likely accept. Then you can increase your prices as needed due to cost of living increases and in accordance with your increased experience. I started out charging a fairly low rate, but as time went by, I realized other editors were successfully charging more—and some were not as qualified or doing as good a job—so I raised my prices. You may want to start out low to build a clientele and get referrals, but over time, as you become more successful, experienced, and in demand, you can raise your prices gradually. In time, you can charge what you are worth and either work fewer hours or just make more money.

Providing a Price Quote for Editing a Book

Here is my formula for figuring out what to charge for a book.

First, determine what your hourly wage will be. Let's go the middle of the road and say you set it at $50 an hour.

Now, open the author's manuscript, turn on the track changes feature, and do a free edit sample. Various editors will suggest different ways to do the edit sample. Some will edit 1,000 words. Some will edit a set number of pages. I generally will edit the entire introduction or first chapter, not to exceed half an hour of my time. Then I'll pick one or two places in the middle of the book to edit. I time myself against the original word count of the passages I edited. Let's say I edited three sections and came up with the following data:

- Introduction: 1,217 words, 27[1] minutes spent editing
- Chapter 6: 814 words, 21 minutes spent editing
- Chapter 13: 989 words, 24 minutes spent editing

An introduction is usually fairly short, so I would edit the whole introduction. For Chapter 6, I might have edited the first few pages. For Chapter 13, I might have edited a few pages at the end of the chapter. I always recommend editing the introduction or first chapter so you get an idea of what the book is about. I also recommend randomly picking one or two other places in the manuscript because sometimes an author will work really hard on an introduction so it might be the most polished part of the book—and not a representative sample. Other times, I find that the author's writing gets better as the book progresses. In any case, you want to get a fair sampling. Note also, authors sometimes assume you read the whole book when you did the sample. I would never do that. It's a huge waste of time if you don't get the job. Just page through, read the chapter titles, and make sure all the needed content is there—you would be surprised how many authors send books that are fragmented and have instructions about adding things that have not been added. This could mean the manuscript will be much longer than it is when you do the sample. Watch for anything like this that might throw off the accuracy of your quote.

In the example above, it took me a total of 72 minutes to do the edit sample. That's a lot of time, especially if the author ends up working with someone else, but you want to make sure your edit sample gives you an accurate estimate of how many hours it will take to edit the book. I recommend taking your time to avoid under- or over-charging. I would say aim for spending 45-60 minutes doing an edit sample.

Remember also, when you do the edit sample, you are not doing it solely to determine how much you will charge. You are also doing it so authors can see what kinds of changes you would make and be sure they feel comfortable working with you. You want to impress the author with what you know and how you would reword sentences so they read better. I

---

1 Note that per *The Chicago Manual of Style,* all numbers under 100 should be written out. However, for the sake of making the mathematical examples here easier to follow, I will use digits throughout this pricing discussion. Situations always arise when it is logical to bend a rule.

always write some comments in the margin of the manuscript (I'm assuming you're using MS Word with the track changes feature on and can insert comments) so the author understands why I changed "who" to "whom" or why I rewrote a sentence.

At the same time, you don't want to overwhelm authors. Find the parts they did well in the sections you edit, even if it's difficult, and write positive comments about them. Don't lie about the quality of their books, but if you can find a good idea, a well-turned phrase, or something highlighting their expertise, compliment it. You want them to know you genuinely care about their work. If nothing else, when you send the quote, let the author know it's a big job and why (to justify your price), but also say that you're up for the job, it's all fixable, and you know that between the two of you, you can create a fantastic book.

Now, based on the time and word count from the sample above, let's do some math.

The three sections you edited total 3,020 words. Divide that by the 72 minutes you spent editing and you come up with 41.9 words per minute. Multiplying 41.9 by 60 minutes gives you the total number of words you'll edit per hour, which comes out to 2,514. You have a 50,000-word manuscript, so divide 50,000 by 2,514 and you get 19.88. It's close enough to round up to 20 hours for your first edit of the manuscript. (Do not be surprised if this number is only 10 hours or even 30 hours or more—it just depends on the quality of the writing.)

I usually do two full edits, edit the author's revisions, and then proofread the book. Ultimately, this is how I would figure out the overall quote, according to how many hours I expect to spend on each part of the process, in the order it happens:

A. 20 hours – first edit
B. 12.5 hours – second edit
C. 2 hours – author revisions
D. 5 hours – proofreading
E. 2 hours – review of layout proofs
— Total: 41.5 hours x $50 per hour = $2,075 for the full edit job.

Let's now look at how I came up with all those numbers.
A. We got this number from the edit sample, as described above.
B. & D. From practice, I know that I can usually proofread 10,000 words in an hour, so the proofreading of a 50,000-word book will take me five hours. (This is provided I edited the book so I already know what's there. If

the proofreading is my first look at the book, it's usually closer to 6,000 words per hour.) I know the second edit will take less time than the first but more than the proofread, so I pick a number halfway between the proofread and first edit, which would be 12.5. I've found this halfway number is relatively accurate for me. I suggest when you do your first quote, you also pick a halfway number, but keep track of how many hours you spend on each part of the process so you can adjust accordingly for future quotes.

C. Typically, authors do some rewriting, which takes me on average about two hours to edit before I proofread. (With track changes, the author's changes will be in a different color, so I can just go page by page editing those changes.) Now, sometimes the second edit takes less time than I expect, but the author might also make more revisions than I expect, so there's a little cushion built in.

Sometimes, the author makes a lot more revisions than I expect, which is why I have a clause in my editing agreement that limits the number of words the author can add before I have to charge for editing those extra words. I usually set the limit at 2,500 or 5,000 words depending on the manuscript's length and the quality of the writing. Once this is exceeded, I charge an hourly rate to edit the new material. I have this clause to give authors leeway to add necessary information for clarity, insert transitions needed for flow, and put in conclusions to help readers understand the overall meaning of the material they just read. I write comments in the margins reminding authors to add these, and once added, they usually amount to a few thousand extra words to edit. That said, some authors will go overboard, rewriting most of the book and adding 10,000 words or more. Editing all those extra words takes time, and I deserve to be paid for that time. So, I build in two hours for author revisions, which allows them some leeway, while my word limit and hourly wage clause protect me from doing hours of extra work for free.

E. The two hours for proof review is time I spend looking at the PDF the layout person sends the author and me to review. Many authors expect you to read the proof, but I never do because, by this point, I've read the book three times and it's not likely I'll find a typo, but I do encourage the authors to read them and send me any corrections they decide they want. I do always page through the proof looking for errors like misspellings in the headers, page numbers on pages that should be blank, widows and orphans (words left hanging by themselves at the top or bottom of a paragraph), or worse, a page that just looks awkward. I encourage authors to read through the proof, putting in sticky notes or highlighting errors (Adobe Acrobat Reader features) in the PDF. (If the author cannot figure out how to put in sticky notes, I ask for a list of corrections and put in the sticky notes myself.) You absolutely have to edit any corrections authors make to the PDF proof because they are likely to create typos with their corrections, and those will end up in the book if you don't catch them. Know going in that layout people rarely read the corrections; they usually just copy and paste whatever they are given. If, as the editor, you don't look over the proofs, I guarantee either the author, layout person, or both will introduce errors into the text. Consequently, I build in time to protect the book from their errors.

So there you have it—how to come up with a price for editing a book. This is a fairly typical quote. I have found that even with well written books, I usually can't edit any faster than 6,000 words an hour—there are always small grammar and punctuation errors to fix, plot issues to question, chronology or organization issues to double-check, or words to look up. I rarely have to look up the spelling of a word or even its definition, but I do spend a lot of time looking up compound nouns to determine whether a word should really be one word, two words, or hyphenated. Words like policyholder, backseat, well-being (some dictionaries prefer well-being), and time frame are the bane of my existence. Why time frame is not one word I will never understand. As for wellbeing, I always make it consistently one word unless the author objects.

You may at this point be wondering how many words per hour the typical editor can edit. No firm answer exists since it will vary according to the book. Most online resources refer to the average number of pages per hour an editor can edit, and these range from four to ten pages with an average page being 250/300 words. Such page number averages are really only useful in ensuring your fees are competitive. You will still need to calculate your price quote using your actual speed and the specific manuscript. And speed is not an indicator of accuracy. I have seen editors who are very fast, but miss a lot, and others who are very slow but do meticulous work and are worth every extra penny you pay them. If you fear you're a little on the slow side, that is okay. You will get faster as you become more experienced, and you may also be catching things other editors are missing. That said, it also helps to strengthen your typing skills. Typing fast has helped me immeasurably. I recommend finding some fun typing games online to help increase your speed and accuracy. Also, the more familiar you are with MS Word, the faster you will be.

Don't be surprised if some books are so rough you can't edit more than a few hundred words per hour. I advise not basing your price on editing anything more than 6,000 words an hour, even for the best book, because something will always slow you down. Now and then, there is the rare book that only needs one edit and a proofread; usually, such a book has already been edited by someone else, but when I look at it, it still needs significant rewriting to fix subject-pronoun agreement issues or reword passive sentences. Rarely have I received a book for proofreading that I didn't think actually needed light editing and that I didn't go through twice, provided the author was agreeable to it—and most have been. Many authors don't know enough about writing to determine how good an editor is, and while I hate pointing out what another editor missed, it is my responsibility to produce as error-free a book as possible, and the author is always grateful for it.

Other Pricing Considerations

While the formula I've shared works for me, I would make two suggestions:

1. Offer a discount for paying in full in advance of work beginning.

If you truly want to make $50 an hour (or whatever hourly wage you decide on), and you offer a discount, then you need to raise your price a little. I offer a 10 percent discount to anyone who pays me in full upfront. Consequently, you might want to change your price to $55 to cover that 10 percent discount—you'll actually get $49.50 if you charge $55. You can offer clients a price based on $55 per hour, and if they opt not to pay in full upfront, you're ahead a few dollars when it's time to get paid, but you also have to wait longer for your money.

I've found it is best to state in your editing agreement that the client has two payment options: 1) Pay in full upfront and get a 10 percent discount, or 2) Pay half upfront and the other half upon completion. Be sure to specify in your editing agreement when completion is. It should be when you send the author the final draft, not when the book goes to layout, the printer, or is listed for sale online. There is no reason for you to wait while the author gets the book laid out, printed, and put on sale. Chances are the author spent three months ignoring the book instead of doing revisions anyway, so six months may have passed since you got your first payment. You don't want to prolong the payment process by waiting for a second payment any longer than you have to.

Ensure you have been clear about when and how you will be paid. The author needs to be clear from the beginning about when the money is due so there is no confusion. Set time frames and limits so you don't have to wait until long after you've done the work to get paid.

I've found that approximately two-thirds of authors will take the discount and pay in full upfront. Most others will make two payments. However, you will also have those who want to make monthly payments. If it's repeat business from people who have paid you on time before, then go ahead and trust them to make payments. If you don't already have a relationship with the author, however, or the author wasn't referred to you by a reliable source, be cautious. I've had authors tell me they'd send me a third upfront, another third a month later, and the final third the following month. This is okay if you have reason to trust the person, but I've been burned by agreeing to such payments more than once.

I once gave a quote for $2,400, and the author agreed to pay me a third upfront, so I was expecting an $800 check. Instead, I got $300. I was halfway through editing by the time the check arrived. I got $200 the next month, and $100 the month after that. Then I got an occasional $100 check every few months before he quit paying and responding to my emails. In the end, I got less than half the agreed upon price while the author got a finished manuscript. I was trusting and it didn't work out. Don't let it happen to you—which brings me to my next point.

2. Accept credit cards.

Initially, I asked clients to mail me checks. Then I would wait…and wait…. Because I had so much work, I would start on their books as soon as I could, not wanting to get backed up and trusting the checks would come. Most of the time they did, but sometimes I would wait three weeks for a check—from people who got the 10 percent upfront payment discount. Making me wait until I'm half-done with the project is not paying upfront. The reason I initially asked for checks was because I didn't want credit card companies to get a cut of my payment, and I certainly didn't want to risk giving out my bank routing number to clients so they could wire me money. However, I got tired of waiting for checks and dealing with the occasional check that bounced. Plus, several clients wanted to pay with their credit cards, so I decided to switch to using PayPal. PayPal takes a 2.9 percent fee, plus $0.03, from any money you receive, so I added 3 percent to my quotes to cover those costs.

Here's how you would figure out what to charge if you wanted to give a 10 percent discount, let clients pay with PayPal, and still make $50 an hour. Add 10 percent to your costs, so charge $55. Then add 3 percent ($1.50 is 3 percent of $50), so you'll charge $56.50 per hour. This math will actually result in you making $49.32 per hour, but it's close enough. Add another dollar or two if you feel the need.

In any case, getting paid upfront through PayPal relieves your stress. The project is paid for and the cash is sitting in your account before you start working on the book.

I know because you're a trustworthy person, you want to assume everyone else is as well, but people will let you down if you give them the opportunity. You're not in the trusting business; you're in the editing business. Let your clients know what to expect and then you'll both be happy. If they don't like your payment terms or pricing, you can always negotiate if you need the work, or you can let them go elsewhere.

Explaining Pricing to Clients

Over the last ten years, I have given editing quotes that have ranged anywhere from $250 (usually for a very short work like a children's book) to more than $6,000. The majority of books fall into the $1,200-$3,000 range. I find that most clients just accept the price I offer them, but once in a while, someone will try to negotiate. Since I instituted the 10 percent discount, that is less frequently the case. However, authors might say, "Why are you charging me $1,800 when my book is only eighty pages?" First off, the book is probably eighty pages in MS Word, but it may be 40,000 words, which, when laid out, could end up being 200 pages, so you can explain that the book is longer than the client thinks. Having an editing agreement helps you deter this question since the client better understands everything you will do.

All that said, sometimes you have to be brutally honest with the author. As nicely as possible, explain the reason for the pricing; for example, "English isn't your first language and that lack of familiarity has caused you to make many errors I will need to fix. I'm only going to be able to edit about 1,200 words an hour, and that means it will take me thirty-three hours just to go through your book once."

Some authors will think they deserve a special price because they're writing a self-help book that will benefit people or they own a nonprofit organization; some will even claim that God told them to write the book. (Yes, I've had a few of those. Oddly enough, God doesn't always provide the funds to pay for the book's editing, or choose someone to write a book who has good writing skills, but maybe God does that so I can have work.) In any case, you're not running a charity. You're trying to feed yourself and your family, pay your mortgage, save for your retirement, and maybe travel the world.

You can be kind without shortchanging yourself by agreeing to multiple payments if you feel the author is trustworthy. At times, it's hard not to lower your price, but over the years, I've become tougher about this, especially after I had a client finagle a discount because he had just lost his job, but a year later, he was vacationing in Australia. I think he could have paid the extra $300 I took off the price.

If you make it clear you're not budging on the price, the client may go elsewhere, but it is more likely you'll get your price. Some clients just want to get a deal. They have the money; they just don't believe in paying full price. That doesn't mean you have to give in to them. If their books are truly important to them, they will pay you what you ask.

No client has ever asked me what my formula is for determining a price, and most don't even ask me what I charge per hour, although I have the price for extra work per hour in my editing agreement. That said, at least once I tried to negotiate with an author who, no matter what price I offered, was not happy. When I came up with a price based on how many hours the work would take, he didn't like it. When I came up with a price based on so many cents per word, he wasn't happy. He just wanted "a price," not one based on anything, which was impossible to do. In the end, he asked me if I could just lower the price by not putting commas in the book because he believed the publishing industry was getting away from using them. I told him I could not do that because I uphold a certain standard for my work. I told him I didn't believe we could work together and wished him well. This incident happened several years ago, and since then, I have yet to see a book published without commas in it, so I guess his predictions about the publishing industry were wrong.

Occasionally, you need to let a bad client or prospect go, regardless of how much you might need the work. Some clients will not be worth whatever price you charge them. We'll discuss such situations further in Chapters 7 and 11. For now, I encourage you to believe that customers are almost always right, but when they are not, I give you permission to fire them.

In the end, you are working for you, and you deserve to be paid what you are worth, so charge accordingly.

Chapter 4
Dotting Your *Is* and Crossing Your *Ts*:
Setting Up Your Business

"You have to work on the business first before it works for you."

— Idowu Koyenikan, *Wealth for All*

N OW THAT YOU' VE decided you have what it takes to become an editor and you can calculate what to charge, you have to be prepared for when the money starts coming in. In other words, you need to have your business set up properly so you don't get in trouble with the IRS or end up spending more than you're making because you're not tracking your cash flow. First, let me say I'm not a financial advisor or an accountant, so while I'll advise you on what you need to do, you'll have to check with professionals on the finer points.

Determining Your Type of Business

The first thing to decide is what kind of business you will have, namely will you be a sole proprietor or an LLC? Most likely, you will be the only owner of your editing business, so there really is no need to investigate other forms of business status. I am a sole proprietor and have found that to be sufficient, although becoming an LLC is not a bad idea, so I'll explain a bit about both options.

To become a sole proprietor, you'll want to visit your local county courthouse's register of deeds office or equivalent (call ahead to save yourself time so you know where to go) and find out how to file for a DBA (Doing Business As). It's a simple form you'll need to fill out stating what your business name is. The cost is minimal. I pay $10 for my DBA status, which is good for five years. By doing this, you are establishing yourself as a business and protecting yourself against others using the same name within your county. Unfortunately, it won't stop others outside your county from using your name, but regardless, you usually need a DBA to open a business bank account.

To fill out the simple DBA form, you will need to have a business name. Be as creative as you want. I initially named my business Superior Book Promotions because, besides editing, I was also writing press releases and book reviews for authors, but over time, I felt I was being pulled in too many directions and decided that editing was going to be my primary focus, so I would leave promoting books to someone else. Consequently, I changed the name to Superior Book Productions. By that point, I had also found a business colleague, Larry Alexander, who was doing websites and book layout. He had his own website, but we thought if we merged to one website and changed the company name, it would better reflect our company's mission and both of our services, plus we could get clients from each other. For your company name, you may want something simpler such as Smith Editing or John Johnson, Editor. It doesn't really matter what you name your company provided the name makes it clear what types of services you provide.

Some people may tell you that you'd be better off becoming an LLC than a sole proprietor. This is certainly something to consider. The primary benefit of being an LLC is that if someone decides to sue you, only your business assets will be at risk and not your personal assets. If this concerns you, then certainly get a lawyer and become an LLC. That said, if you have a straightforward editing agreement and you abide by the terms of that agreement, you should never have a problem with an unhappy client. I tend to bend over backwards for my clients and do more than they expect to keep them happy. I've never been in a situation yet where a client threatened to sue me, and if I ever should be, I would offer to refund the client's money to avoid a lawsuit. I can't imagine, honestly, why anyone would sue an editor other than for failure to complete the work, so if you're a reliable editor, you shouldn't have a problem.

Sometimes authors get sued for libel over a memoir, so I suppose you could be party to the dispute as the editor. This is extremely unlikely, however, and again, if you're a good editor, you will warn your client about anything that might be considered libel and also tell the client to consult a lawyer. (It's best to give such advice in an email rather than over the phone so you have a written record.) If clients have issues after that, it's on them. For these reasons, I don't think forming an LLC is necessary, but if you feel your situation requires you to protect your business, it might be worth paying the fees and filing the paperwork for your peace of mind.

Most people will tell you to keep your business and your personal funds separate. That said, I've never worried about this since I'm the sole proprietor and all my business income is my personal income. However, you should go to your bank with your DBA paperwork and set up a business account anyway. If you want to go through the process of depositing all your income into your business account and then writing checks to yourself, you can certainly do that. However, the only reason I have a business checking account is for the few clients who write checks payable to Superior Book Productions, even though my invoices say to make the checks payable to Tyler Tichelaar. If they do that, and you do not have an account in your company name, the bank will refuse to cash the check. Frankly, it's a pain to have the other account, but regardless, I go to the bank to deposit the checks in my business account, and then I go online and transfer the funds from my business to my personal account.

Bookkeeping

You'll also need a system for keeping track of your income and expenses. A simple Microsoft Excel spreadsheet should be sufficient; however, many prefer accounting software like QuickBooks. I've found that a spreadsheet has always worked for me. I have one page that has columns for the following categories and looks like this:

Client Name	Book Title	Service	Payment	Date	Status
John Smith	My Novel	Editing	$1,500	May 14, 2018	Paid ½ of $3,000
Mary Jones	My Memoir	Editing	$1,970	May 20, 2018	Paid in Full
Mark White	Poems	Proofread-ing	$300	May 22, 2018	Paid in Full

I have another page in my spreadsheet for expenses. I break these down into the following eight categories (also in columns). I'll explain each category's purpose.

1. **Editing:** Because Larry works with me editing clients' books, I track any money I pay him for editing in this column. Because the client pays me, which is income, and then I pay Larry for doing part of the work, an expense offsetting part of the income, payments to Larry are an expense I have to track.

2. **Equipment:** This includes anything I purchase such as a new laptop, software for my computer, paper, or ink for my printer.

3. **Events:** This section is for conferences or events I might attend. I also keep track of business lunches in this category.

4. **Internet/Web:** I pay Larry to maintain my website. I also pay for my domain names, website hosting, and internet service.

5. **Marketing:** I might occasionally take out an ad online or in a print publication to advertise my services. I also have business cards, brochures, etc. printed. If I pay a referral fee, I also record it under this category.

6. **Postage:** On the rare occasion that I have to mail something for my business, I have a postage column. (I actually spend a lot of money on postage, but since I'm also an author, it is for mailing my own books that people have ordered from me.)

7. **Taxes:** This category is for the money I pay my accountant.

8. **Travel:** These are expenses incurred while traveling to conferences or other business-related events. I also keep track of mileage in a separate column since the government will give you credit for work-related mileage. Each year the rate for mileage changes, but your accountant should know what it is. In 2014, it was .56 cents per mile. In 2018, it was .545 cents. Since you work from home, you probably won't drive for work-related purposes too much. I typically drive around 1,000 miles per year for work-related purposes and most of that is related to book deliveries and author events, but as an editor, you might have business lunches with clients or have to run to Office Max to buy ink for your printer, and all those little trips should be tracked. Every penny counts when running a business, so getting $500 worth of credit for my mileage is definitely worth keeping track of. I also understand that if you lease your car and use it for business, you can write off your payments. Check with your accountant on this or any other expenses you think might qualify as a business expense. (Note that I don't bother to figure out how many dollars' worth of mileage I should receive a credit on my taxes for. I just keep track of the mileage and give the total to my accountant at the end of the year. I don't figure it into my calculations for my quarterly taxes, as explained below.)

Now that you have all your expense columns in place, total the costs in each column and then give those numbers to your accountant.

You'll also have to pay quarterly taxes to state and federal governments, so you'll need to keep track of what your expenses and income are each quarter. I have a formula in my spreadsheet set up to subtract my expenses from my income and come up with my net income after expenses. This number is then used to determine what I owe in taxes. Let's say my income for the quarter, after expenses, was $10,000. I then multiply it by 20 percent to determine what I owe in federal taxes and by 3 percent (.03) for my state taxes, so if for the quarter I clear $10,000 after deducting my expenses, I would pay $2,000 in taxes to the federal government and $300 to the state government. Note the percentages I pay are what my accountant and I determined would be most accurate for me. Percentages you should pay will depend on your income tax bracket and your state.

I pay my taxes quarterly to the government using this formula and then meet with my accountant during tax season with the details of all my expenses, income, and other items such as bank interest, utility payments, percentage of my home that can be written off for business use, etc. to determine what I owe the government or it owes me. I've been using this system for many years and paying those percentages to the government quarterly based on my accountant's advice. Each year, I usually come out owing or receiving back somewhere around $0-300, which means, basically, there are no big surprises for me or the government.

I cannot stress enough how important it is to find a good accountant who is skilled at doing taxes for business owners and especially sole proprietors. Do not just go to some discount tax preparation service that may have no experience doing business taxes. I went to a well-known, large tax service company the first year I was in business, and while the person I worked with was kind enough to explain everything to me, which helped me understand what expenses to track and how to categorize them, I ended up paying over $500. I then asked a few friends for recommendations—be sure you ask other people who own their own businesses—and I found someone I've used ever since who does my taxes for $80. I have everything in order when I go to his office, and I'm in and out of there in less than an hour. When I leave, I know exactly what I owe or have coming back. Since my accountant used to work for the IRS, I'm confident he knows what he's doing. You may not find anyone that inexpensive where you live, but do your research and make sure you get someone qualified.

I advise using an accountant rather than doing your own taxes because if there's a mistake, you have your accountant to help you, and hopefully, he or she will know how to deal with the IRS to get the problem resolved. And trust me, both the state and federal governments will make mistakes and send you what might be perceived as threatening letters. Almost every year, the State of Michigan claims it didn't get one of my payments. I can handle this situation myself simply by letting it know the check number of the check I sent and the date the check was cashed. The IRS once sent me a letter saying I hadn't claimed income from a client who sent me a $75,000 payment. I wish I earned that much per book, but the IRS' scanner had simply misread the W-2 the client sent as $75,000 instead of $750.00. My accountant sent a letter to the IRS for me and the situation was easily resolved. It's important not to freak out when you get such letters. They may be a bit intimidating, but I have yet to be audited or have any real problems. As long as you are honest about everything and keep a paper trail, you won't have problems either.

Make sure you ask your accountant to write off part of your home as office space. Measure the area you use for your office space and give it to your accountant. Ideally, you should have a separate room in the house. I have a couple of rooms—one I work in, and one where all my books are stored—both my personal library, which I use as research for writing my own books, and my inventory of books to sell. Give your accountant the measurement of the room(s) and the full square footage of your home. From this, he can calculate the percentage of your home you can write off. You will also need to keep track of your mortgage payments, mortgage interest, and utility payments because the percentage of those payments that equal the percentage of your office space also get written off. Note, you cannot write off a room with a bed in it, but you can if you have a futon or a hide-a-bed. If you have an accountant who refuses to write off part of your home, find another accountant.

Keep all your business receipts just in case you should get audited. With taxes, save everything for at least seven years. I use a small box like a shoebox and dump all my receipts in it, as well as stubs from any checks I receive, invoice copies, etc. Then I have them just in case I'm ever audited. That said, be sure you have some sort of system for logging all your receipts, like I described above, so you have them divided into categories and always know the totals. Neither you nor your accountant will want to wade through a few hundred receipts at the end of the year.

Retirement Funds

Now that you're working for yourself, you won't be contributing to a 401k. But that doesn't mean you have to let your money sit in the bank where you will only earn pennies in interest. Find a financial advisor who can roll over your 401k money from your previous job. Then open a Roth IRA and try to max it out every year. As of 2019, the maximum you can put in a Roth IRA is $6,000 per year if you're under age fifty and an additional $1,000 if you're fifty or older. If you can afford to, open a Simple IRA also. A Roth IRA is a personal IRA that allows you to defer taxes. A Simple IRA is a personal business account. You can put up to $13,000 per year in it if you're under fifty and an additional $3,000 if you're fifty or older. After that, you can also consider mutual funds or annuities. Again, I'm not a financial advisor, but I will tell you that a Roth and a Simple IRA are the way to go.

If you don't have these accounts yet, get them as soon as possible and then monthly set money aside for them. Contribute to your Roth IRA first and max it out if you can. If you still have additional money, put it in your Simple IRA. Since you are self-employed, you may not want to set up automatic payments to your retirement accounts because your income may be volatile at times, especially early on in your freelance career, but try to put aside at least 10 percent of your income as you receive it so you are prepared for your retirement.

Have an Emergency Fund

I also recommend that you set aside part of your savings for an emergency fund. The financial experts will tell you to have six to ten months of income set aside in case of emergencies—for you, an emergency might be a broken arm that makes it impossible to type so you can't edit, or it might be a lack of work that means you have to live off your savings for a month or two.

Remember also, since you are working for yourself, you'll be paying for all of your own health insurance. Be forewarned that health insurance costs continue to rise rapidly and there are no good and affordable plans out there for the self-employed. You will probably not be able to afford the best coverage available; more likely, you'll opt for a plan with a low monthly fee and a high deductible that might be in the area of $5,000 or more. As a result, you'll want to set aside $5,000 or whatever dollar amount is appropriate in your emergency fund in case you have medical expenses. And believe me, no matter how healthy you are, the day will come when you will need it. I exercise regularly, try to eat right, and hardly ever get a cold, but that didn't stop my appendix from rupturing. Six days in the hospital and a $40,000 bill later, I was grateful I had put aside enough money in my emergency fund to pay my $5,000 deductible.

So set aside an emergency fund first. Then set money aside for your re-tirement. I can't stress these two items enough. You are working as an editor not for fun but so you have money to pay your bills, and you want to be able to pay your bills if you are ill and also when you are older and not working anymore. You might also want to look into disability insurance in case you become injured and cannot work. I have a mortgage disability policy that will pay my mortgage monthly up to three years should I become unable to work. Funny thing is, I paid off my mortgage years ago, but my insurance company lets me keep the policy and will still pay me monthly if I become disabled. I keep the policy since it only costs me about $250 a year and gives me security.

If you are the sole proprietor of your editing business, you are your big-gest asset—protect that asset. You get no paid vacation time or sick leave. Live a healthy lifestyle and protect yourself financially if you become ill. You are not working for your health but for your financial wellbeing, so save your money and then you won't be caught off-guard when an emergency arises. And as I said, it will....

Now that you know how to set up your business, it's time to find some clients so you can make money to live on, save for emergencies, save for re-tirement, and live like a nomad if you choose; therefore, in the next chapter, we'll talk about how to market yourself.

Chapter 5
Look World, Here I Am:
Marketing Your Business

*"A brand for a company is like a reputation for a person.
You earn reputation by trying to do hard things well."*

— Jeff Bezos, Founder of Amazon

N<small>OW THAT YOU</small> have everything in place, it's time to drum up some business for yourself. In other words, it's time to find some clients. If you're an introvert, marketing yourself can be hard to do, but don't despair. If you're passionate about your business (if you're not, you're in the wrong business) and you can express that passion to others, I guarantee work will come your way.

When I became an author, one of the first things I did was read John Kremer's *1001 Ways to Market Your Book*. In it, Kremer states, "Book marketing is all about creating friends." Guess what—so is marketing your editing business and networking and all other forms of business marketing. What you want to do is make a few friends who will help promote you. Before you know it, those few friends will attract more friends to you.

You can make friends in so many ways. Begin by conveying a professional yet friendly demeanor in everything you do to market yourself. Make all your marketing materials friendly and engaging, and most of all, remember that your purpose is to help authors make friends with their readers by helping them create first-rate books. Befriend authors and they will repay you with work.

Following are the primary areas you will want to dedicate your marketing efforts toward.

Website

First and foremost, you need a website. People want to see who you are, get an idea of your qualifications, and learn what you do.

Your website doesn't have to be fancy. You could use WordPress or templates or whatever is inexpensive and simple when you start off. I began using iPower and its templates when I built my first website because the templates were simple and meant I didn't need to know HTML. Eventually, though, I became frustrated with the templates' limitations, so I had Larry build a website for me and then teach me the basics of using Dreamweaver so I could update my website. However, as time went by, I found it frustrating to update my website because I made changes to it so infrequently that I couldn't remember how to do the things I needed to do to make a change; it would take me three times as long to update it as it did when Larry did it. That was time taken from editing books, so I was losing money updating my website. As a result, eventually, I turned the website over to Larry and now just pay him to update it as needed.

When you're starting your business, you may have time to create your own website since you don't yet have many clients. You also may not want to spend money if you don't have money coming in, so it makes sense to do it yourself. As time goes on, however, you'll find it's best to focus on your strengths and let others help you where you need help, which is what I learned to do.

If you visit my website www.SuperiorBookProductions.com, you'll see it has numerous pages and is rather complex in its structure. That's because my company provides other services besides editing, such as websites, book layout, and book reviews. I post all the book reviews I write to the site, and over time, that has resulted in several hundred book reviews. I post the reviews there because frequent new content helps search engines find me and it gives extra exposure to my clients' books. I also send out a newsletter every month or two in which I promote the book reviews. This newsletter goes to all of my former editing clients as well as all my readers. I also use it to promote my own books, so I'm exposing my clients' books to those who have opted to receive my mailings because they are interested in books. I also have a blog where I write articles about editing, language, writing, grammar, etc., because if someone is looking for an editor or an author is simply googling something like what is the proper use of who vs. whom and I have an article on my site about it, the author might think, "Who is this guy?" or even notice that I do editing and hire me.

In time, you may expand your website to contain as many features and as much content as mine currently has. For now, however, since you're just starting out, a simple website with basic information should work. Be sure to have a section about yourself that gives your biography and qualifications as an editor. Then have another section describing the services you offer, what you charge, etc. Note that you don't want to post specific prices on your website, but you can give a range and clarify that you will provide an edit sample and customized bid because every book is different. All your customer really wants to know is whether you're qualified and an idea of what it will cost, so that's all you need on your website. All that said, the more professional you can make your site look, the better.

Unfortunately, with websites too many people buy into the line from the movie *Field of Dreams*, "If you build it, they will come." No, they really won't. Maybe a few authors will stumble upon your website, but it isn't likely to get too many clients in the door by itself. What it will do is serve as a place you can refer people to so they can find out more about your services, and it's a place your friends can tell people to go to, but, bottom line, if people don't know your website exists, they aren't likely to go there. Sure, some will find you doing a Google search, but most won't. I seriously doubt even 10 percent of my editing clients have come to me because of my website. Those who have hired me after finding it are usually people who live in the Marquette, Michigan, area, are looking for someone local, and have googled something like "editors in Upper Michigan." Since Marquette has 20,000 people, there's only a handful of authors here who need my help. If you live in New York City, there are doubtless thousands of authors who need your help, but there are also dozens of editors, so what's the chance your website will be the one an author will find? In other words, don't rely on your website to bring you business. Instead, get out there and promote yourself. I've listed several ways below.

Advertising

I'll tell you right now not to waste your money on advertising. I've advertised in newspapers, magazines, and anthologies and received little if any return for it. I've also advertised using Facebook ads without any success. There are too many ways to get free publicity and promote yourself at little or no cost to waste money on advertising. Just don't do it.

Social Media

Social media can be an editor's best friend. Thousands, if not millions, of authors are on Twitter and Facebook alone, so go out and find them. I personally dislike Twitter and rarely use it, but I am active on Facebook. If you're not on Facebook, you're missing a huge opportunity to make people aware of who you are and what you do. Create a personal Facebook page, and then if you want, create one for your editing business as well. I guarantee that someone you know on Facebook is writing a book or interested in writing a book and could benefit from your help. Furthermore, everyone you know from high school, college, past jobs, etc. will think, "Wow, Joanne is now an editor and works from home. How cool is that!" People think being a freelance editor is a dream job so they won't forget it's what you do, and when they meet people writing books and looking for editors, they'll send them to you.

LinkedIn is another great site to be on—it's the most professional of the social media sites, so it's where people may well find you if they're looking for an editor. People now treat LinkedIn and Facebook like they do email—as a way to do business, so if you don't have profiles at these sites, you are losing out on opportunities to make money. Just be sure to check your social media pages at least once a day so you respond to people who decide to contact you through them in a timely manner.

Facebook also has many groups for authors and publishers, so join some of these groups and get involved. Do not go into these groups overtly trying to sell your services, but if someone asks a question, you can say, "As an editor, my opinion is…." to let them know you are qualified to help them. These are all ways to get the word out that you can provide a service people are looking for without trying to sound like you're self-promoting.

Networking

Beyond social media, there are plenty of writing and publishing groups you can join, many right in your city or neighborhood. Google the name of your state and "publishing organizations" to find the ones near you. Join these organizations and get involved in them. Most of the members will be authors, often self-published ones, who will likely need an editor. Again, don't go into these groups trying to sell your services, but get to know people and be interested in their books; then you're likely to come away with a client.

It was by joining the Upper Peninsula Publishers and Authors Association that I met Patrick Snow, who came to be the guest speaker for our organization's annual conference. That one connection has brought me a couple of hundred editing clients. I have also edited books for several of the members in our organization and found fellow authors to exchange manuscripts with to get feedback for my own writing. In addition, I've served as both vice-president and president of the organization, given presentations at our conferences, planned our conferences, and helped plan many local author book events. Get involved, get to know people, and make friends. People do business with people they like, so if you're their friend, they will refer clients to you or become your clients themselves.

Be sure when you join a group that you make friends not just with the authors but also with others who provide services to authors such as local printers, layout people, and web designers. Many of the authors in the group may only have one book to edit, but don't discount that because those authors can refer other authors to you even if they won't be giving you repeat business. However, other service providers may well refer multiple people to you. I've worked with a printer who frequently refers authors to me whose manuscripts are in need of editing before their books are laid out and printed. A website person is less likely to refer an author to you, since most authors will have their books written and even printed before they realize they need a website, but you can make connections with web developers you can refer your editing clients to so they can have websites made for their books. Ask web developers whether they are willing to pay you a referral fee (10 percent is fairly standard) for every client you refer and tell them you'll return the favor.

What you are doing in these situations, as I said before, is not just networking, but making friends. People do business with people they like, so if you can find service people you like and who like you, you can mutually benefit.

Other people who provide book-related services whom you might consider making contacts with include typists, computer repair people, indexers, illustrators, and graphic design artists. As I noted earlier, I hit gold when I befriended publishing coach Patrick Snow, and he's sent me a steady stream of clients for years as a result. I've also done editing for my friend Victor Volkman, whom I met through the *Authors Access* internet radio show. He owns his own publishing company, Loving Healing Press, and sends me work on a fairly regular basis. You never know who might become a good contact, so let everyone know you're an editor. Your financial advisor may have a regular blog or newsletter, but he may not be the world's greatest writer, so he might pay you to edit it for him. I edit blogs for several people, all of whom are authors I first edited books for. Their blogs only take a few minutes to edit, and I usually only charge them ten dollars to edit one, but if you have someone asking you to edit a blog every week, that's $520 a year of guaranteed income. Editing a blog for ten minutes or so a week won't interrupt your schedule much, and it'll buy you a few weeks' worth of groceries by year's end.

Online Freelance Sites

Many websites exist for freelancers looking for work and people looking for freelancers. When I first became an editor, I had accounts at LimeExchange (now Freelancer) and guru.com. Unfortunately, I never got any work from these sites. People would continually post jobs, but the job postings would frequently read something like, "I need someone to write five 500-word book reviews for $20." In other words, they are low paying jobs for less than minimum wage (think how many hours it would take to read five books and write reviews of them) that are usually being outsourced to people in foreign countries. That said, go ahead and sign up at these sites just to see what might happen. You only need to find one good client at a site and that person might refer you to countless other good clients. Today, one of the more reliable sites is www.upwork.com. I know a few editors who are listed there. I personally am not listed on any of these sites any longer because I have more work than I can keep up with, but in the beginning, it was worth making the effort.

Word-of-Mouth

Word-of-mouth is absolutely the best way to promote your business. First of all, make sure you have business cards printed. When you go places, always have business cards to hand out, and take every opportunity to tell people what you do. When I go to the bank, the tellers frequently say to me, "Are you done working today?" or "How is your day going?" and I say, "No, I'm always working, but I get to work from home so it's great" or "It's a busy day. I have a book I'm proofreading that I have to finish today." Saying simple things like this will let them know you're an editor and give them the opportunity to remark, "Oh, I'm writing a book" or "My sister is writing a book," or "I've always wanted to write a book." Then tell them, "Well, if you need help, give me a call" and give them your card.

I cannot stress enough here not to be shy. People are interested in what you do. If you don't promote yourself, how are you going to get other people to promote you? Trust me, I am a huge introvert, but I have learned to save being an introvert for when I'm at home. When I go outside, I put on my extroverted, friendly editor/author smile. I've come to realize that anywhere I am can be an author event because someone in my small city will likely know me and introduce me to other people as an author and those people may think it's a big deal to meet an author—it feels like an event to them. Author or editor, people will think you can help them or their friends with the books they are writing, so never be afraid to confess who you are and promote your services. I have yet to have anyone tell me to shut up just for mentioning what I do. Once I tell people what I do, I leave it up to them whether they want to question me about it. I try not to be pushy with my services, but I'm always open to talking about them to anyone who wants to hear how I might be able to help.

Of course, the best word-of-mouth you'll receive is from past clients who are happy with the job you did. They will sing your praises and refer other people to you. In case you haven't figured it out by now, somewhere around half the population thinks about writing a book. As an author myself, when I do a book signing or go to a craft show to sell my books, I guarantee at least one person will talk to me about how to get a book published. Now, you may be saying, "But I'm not an author." No worries; you don't have to be, because all those people you edited books for are authors and they have people asking them, "Mary, how'd you do it? How'd you publish that book?" and Mary will say, "I had a great editor who helped me, and then he pointed me to a great layout person. Here, let me write down his name and phone number for you." You can't pay for advertising like that. Most authors love to talk about their books and their writing and publishing processes, and they are very willing to help other people who want to write books to fulfill their dreams of being published.

Guess what? As an editor, you are in the "making-dreams-come-true" business. No, you don't need to wear fairy wings or have a magic wand, but you are the person helping an author fulfill a dream—and not just the dream of writing a book, but the dream of sharing that book with the world—a book that might help someone learn to recover from drug addiction, or lose weight, or build a business, or simply relax and laugh for an hour to reduce stress. And because we editors are in the "making-dreams-come-true" business, the people we help love us and are usually in a very good mood. They're not pissed off at you because your prices went up or you quit offering their favorite burger. They're thrilled that you're helping them become published authors, and you should be thrilled that, in helping them, you're helping to make the world a better place.

Editing is a win-win for everyone when you do it well, and word-of-mouth referrals are proof that you are.

However, to get those great word-of-mouth referrals, you need to keep your customers happy, the subject of our next chapter.

Chapter 6
Wow, You're Fast!:
Setting and Exceeding Expectations

"Successful people are always looking for opportunities to help others. Unsuccessful people are always asking, 'What's in it for me?'"

— Brian Tracy

S ALESPEOPLE WILL TELL you that we're all in sales, and that's completely true, but we're also all in customer service. No matter how fabulous your sales skills may be, sales won't last if you don't provide excellent customer service.

As an editor, you have to be prepared to go the extra mile for your clients as often as possible, but you also have to learn how to protect your time and not do things for free that you should be paid for.

When you initially sell yourself to a client, you want to be very responsive, but don't be responsive simply to get the sale. Too many people are extra-friendly and helpful until the customer hands over the money, and then the quality of the service declines. Don't let that situation describe you. You need to treat your clients the way you want to be treated, and never forget that authors think of their books as their children, so you have to keep them convinced throughout the editing and publishing journey that you are the best person possible to take care of their children and do for those children what they cannot do themselves.

When I became an editor, I envisioned having wonderful novels I would get to edit and comment on—and fix typos in. I had no idea I would end up editing four or five self-help or business books for every novel I would get to edit, and I had no idea that most people could not write almost as well as I could. Unlike me, most people who write self-help and business books have not been aspiring novelists since age nine; in fact, they may not have written much of anything since they were in college or even high school until they had the idea to write a book. Consequently, their writing skills may be weak—and they may or may not know it. Regardless, you have to win them over by convincing them that you can improve their books and they have books worth editing and publishing.

Never lie to your clients, but be tactful when being honest. If a client's manuscript is really rough, I say it is rough, but I also say it's fixable and that I can fix it. Now and then, a manuscript may be so rough I have to ask for an exorbitant amount of money. I have at times asked for more than $6,000 to edit a book because it was really long or really poorly written and would take a long time to fix. I've only had one author agree to a quote that size, and his book was just very long and not badly written at all, but I have done several books that have been between $3,000 and $4,000. By contrast, the average book I edit tends to run $1,200-$3,000. When you ask someone for that much money, you have to prove your services are worth it.

The best way to convince clients they need you is, when they first contact you, to tell them to send you their manuscripts as MS Word documents. Then explain, "I'll do a free edit sample for you of a few pages in different places so you can see what kinds of changes I would make or suggestions I would have, and that way you can make sure you're comfortable with my work; also, based on that sample, I can come up with a price and time frame for you." In other words, you're letting clients know upfront that you don't expect them to pay for something sight unseen. While the edit sample is done partly so I can determine a price, it's also done so clients will have an idea of what they are paying for. Here is your first opportunity to show clients how you will care for their books and convince them they need you.

When doing an edit sample, you need to prove your worth. With some books, that's very easy, but with others, it can be a little challenging. If it's a poorly written book, you can easily turn the track changes on and then re-write nearly every sentence in the sample passages to show what needs to be done. A well-written book may only require insertion of a few commas and fixing a few typos in your edit sample. That's okay. A well-written book was written by an author who largely knows how to write and who will value your comma or your one grammatical change. That author will also appreciate the relatively low price you'll charge because the work won't take you long. An edit sample for a poorly written book will look like a string of red marks and be nearly impossible to read, but all those corrections will probably shock authors into realizing they need you. Beyond that, I always write comments in the margins explaining why I'm making changes. Some of those comments might read like this:

- I added these three words to clarify the point you are making because I was a little confused here. Make sure this says what you meant.
- Writing in all caps is considered shouting at the reader and it is also hard to read. Anything you want to emphasize should be italicized instead. That said, use italics sparingly. Italicizing words on every page or in every paragraph takes away from their significance.
- I wrote in this sentence to provide a better transition between these paragraphs, but feel free to reword it as you see fit.
- As Stephen King says, "The adverb is not your friend," so I removed "nonchalantly." When you write dialogue, it's best to stick to dialogue tags like "said," "replied," and "asked" and leave out the adverb. The words spoken by the character make it clear from the tone that the character is being nonchalant so there's no need for the adverb.

In other words, you are explaining to clients why you are making changes, but you are also selling them on why they need you since they likely didn't realize such a change was needed. I usually write numerous comments like this in the edit sample, then assume the author understands when I correct similar errors so I don't need to write such comments throughout the book. Most authors will make the same recurring errors, so there's no need to explain why you changed the pronouns every time.

Along with the edit sample, I always send an editing agreement outlining the entire editing process. This way clients know exactly what to expect, and they sign the agreement to show they agree with it. This agreement also ensures you get paid for extra work if the client later ends up rewriting the book to an extreme. Below is my typical editing agreement. (Note: Everything underlined in the agreement is what I change for each individual client. Not underlined but also changed at times is the 5,000 words designation. Depending on the writer and length of the book, I might adjust this down to 2,500 words or raise it to no higher than 10,000. I try to ensure it is not more than two extra hours of work for me.)

Superior Book Productions Editing Agreement

This price quote and agreement is for editing and proofreading of a book titled *My Book* by Jane Parker. It constitutes an agreement between said author and Tyler R. Tichelaar and staff, dba Superior Book Productions, located at 1202 Pine St., Marquette, MI 49855.

This agreement is based upon the following expectations concerning process and work to be performed.

Manuscript Expectations

The manuscript, at time of submission to the editor, is a length of <u>62,500 words, to include the main manuscript and extra insert pages (Dedication, Acknowledgments, About the Author, Sales Pages, Testimonials, and Book Cover text)</u>. Any changes by the author to the manuscript after this agreement is established in excess of 5,000 words will result in an additional fee at the rate of $50.00 per hour for editing and proofreading of the changes.

The Editing and Book Production Process

The editor and author both agree to the following process for preparing the book for publication.

1. The editor(s) will make two complete edits to the manuscript. These edits will be done consecutively, unless after the first edit, the editor feels it is best to return the book to the author to do some revisions prior to the second edit. On the first edit, the editor will fix all grammar and punctuation and spelling errors. The editor will also read to get the big picture of the book. On the second edit, the editor will make comments and revisions, focus on organization and content, and write suggestions for the author to make changes as desired. Some of these items will happen simultaneously during both edits as needed.

2. The author will read through the edited manuscript and make any changes desired based on the editor's suggestions, revisions, and professional opinion. It is understood that the book is the property of the author so all final decisions are the author's. The author may take as long as needed to make the revisions.

3. The author will return the revised manuscript to the editor, who will then edit the author's revisions for grammar, punctuation, and content as soon as possible based on the editor's workload at the time the

book is returned, or based on any agreement made between the editor and author, as long as the author has returned the revised book when expected. The editor will then inform the author whether the manuscript needs any more additions or revisions or whether the manuscript is ready to be proofread. If additional revisions are necessary, the editor will return the manuscript to the author to do so. Excessive revisions constituting more than 5,000 words will be edited at the rate of $50.00 per hour for the editor's time.

4. Once a second round of revisions is completed by the author, the editor will edit the revisions and then proofread the book.

5. Once the book is proofread, the editor will then submit the proofread manuscript to the book design and layout person. (Note that you will need to hire a layout person to design your book. Layout is not included within the editing quote.) The editor submits the book to the layout person to prevent a situation where the author decides to make changes and forgets to inform the editor of them so they are not edited or proofread. The author agrees that once the book goes to the layout person, no more rewriting will be done beyond fixing obvious typos or errors introduced during the layout process. If the author decides to rewrite anything during the layout process, any time the editor spends on revisions after the layout is complete will be billed at the rate of $50.00 per hour.

6. The editor will also assist the author in drafting or editing the cover/book jacket pieces, including a book description, author bio, any sales pages, and any testimonials acquired.

7. Once the book is laid out, the layout person will send the author and editor a PDF of the laid out pages. The author and editor will then look over the PDF to make sure the book is ready for printing. Since the book has already been proofread, the editor is not required to proofread it again at this stage, but the editor will look for formatting and layout issues, including any typos in titles, headers, or other items the layout person may have adjusted. The author may read the entire book if desired, but only formatting and obvious errors or typos should be corrected at this point. The author will send all desired corrections to the editor, who will combine all corrections as comments in the PDF for the layout person. The editor will also double-check all the layout person's corrections to ensure accuracy before the manuscript goes to the printer.

Payment Terms
The editor agrees to provide all the services listed above for the sum of
$2,350.00 USD.
Two payment options are available:
The author pays half upfront and the remaining half after the book is proof-read and before it is released to the layout person.
The author can make a payment in full upfront and receive a 10 percent discount.
PayPal is the preferred method of payment. The editor will send the author a payment request. Other payment arrangements can be made if necessary. Editing will begin once the first payment is made.
The author agrees to all the terms of this agreement and will return to the editor a signed paper or electronic copy by postal mail or email.

Signature of Author _____ **Date** _____

Signature of Editor _____ **Date** _____

Note that I always make whatever changes needed per individual book in the MS Word template I have for this agreement. Then I create a PDF to send to the author to sign. I use a PDF so the author cannot make changes to the agreement. However, if the author wants any changes, I am open to discussing them. For example, sometimes an author only wants a one-time proofread, or to make multiple payments, or a confidentiality clause. If needed, I will add such details to the agreement and then send a new copy for the author to sign.

When I send the edit sample and editing agreement to the author, I also always make a point of telling the author how long it will take me to return the manuscript, and I promise to provide updates as I go along and let the author know if I have any questions. (Note that I never put a date in the editing agreement for when I will return a manuscript because life can get in the way, or more likely, the book may turn out to be more work than I expected. I don't promise anything I'm not sure I can deliver.) Depending on the book and other projects I'm working on, I will usually tell the author it will take two or three weeks to do the two main edits and return the manuscript. Occasionally, I ask for longer, depending on the book. I also let the author know that after a week, I'll send an email with a progress update. If I've finished a complete edit by that point, I'll ask any questions I might have. It never hurts to ask a question or two because that lets the author know you're working on the book and you're engaged in the process. At the very least, I will send an email letting authors know of anything they might want to work on while I finish my work. Because authors often forget about all the peripheral pieces of a book, I'll usually send an email that says something like:

Hi Jane,
While I'm finishing up my work, I thought I'd let you know a few pieces are missing you might want to write up and send to me when you get a chance. Namely:

- **Dedication page:** Keep this short—usually just one sentence or line, such as "To George, who was always there for me."
- **Acknowledgments page:** This page lists everyone who helped or supported you in writing the book. It can be just a list of names or it can be a sentence or two thanking each person for something specifically.
- **About the Author page:** Write this page in third person about yourself and make it about three paragraphs long. Tell us anything you think will make you look like an authority on your subject and that will make the reader interested in you. (You can consult other books for examples of these first three items.)
- **Sales pages:** These are pages to put in the back of the book for topics like "Hire Jane Parker to Speak at Your Next Event" or "Experience the Magic of Parker Consulting" or "Be Sure to Read All of Jane Parker's Books."
- **Back cover text:** I will help you make this perfect, but if you could write up a draft of about 250 words that clarifies what the book is about, why it's of value, and why the reader needs it, that will help me know how you see your book and want to promote it, and then I can polish it up for you.

Thank you. Let me know if you have questions.
Tyler

All these pages need to be written anyway, and they really aren't something you as the editor can write for the author (except the back cover text, which I often just write myself, but it never hurts to ask the author to take a first stab at it). I also will often send sample pages of the sales pages to nudge the author along. By asking authors to work on these pieces, you are making them feel thankful that you know what you're doing and that you are looking out for them by letting them know what they need to do next. We'll discuss the actual wording of these pages in Chapter 14.

Once I've finished editing the manuscript, I always send an email that explains what I'm sending back to the client. That email will read something like this:

Hi Jane,
Here is your manuscript back. I'm attaching:

1. **Edited Copy:** This shows all the changes made—it's rather a mess to look at, so I suggest you just use it as a reference if you want to see a specific change I made, or you may be better off just looking at your original manuscript for comparison.
2. **Clean Copy:** This version is the same as the edited one except I accepted all of the changes so it would be easier to read. I made so many changes it would have been difficult for you to make sense of the edited copy. Use this one so you can focus on what the book says now and not every comma or word I changed. All my comments are still in this version so you'll know what major changes I made or what suggestions I have. Make all your changes in this version. The track changes feature is turned on so I will be able to see everything you change.
3. **Notes:** This document outlines some of the major things I changed or that you need to change or make decisions on.

I recommend you:

1. Read the Notes document.
2. Page through the Clean Copy and read all my comments so you get the big picture of what needs to be done.
3. Go ahead and make your revisions.
4. Send the file back to me when you finish and then I'll go through all your edits and let you know if anything else is needed. Then I'll do the proofreading.

Take as long as you need to make your revisions and let me know if you have any questions.
Have fun working on it!
Tyler

I recommend that you keep scripts for all the emails you will be sending regularly. Of course, you can edit and personalize them for each client as needed, but in general, you'll be telling each client the same thing. Save yourself from retyping the same information every time. I have templates for the "To Do" and "Manuscript Return" emails where I just have to change the author's name in the greeting line. I also have one explaining how to mark up the PDF once the book is laid out that I'll share below. Of course, sometimes these will vary—the author might have an acknowledgments page already, so I'll delete that line, or I might not return an edited and a clean copy because the author's book is so well-written it was basically just a proofreading job so the edited version is sufficient.

I began sending the clean copy version of the manuscript to authors to make their lives and mine easier. Books that are heavily rewritten or heavily edited are nearly impossible to read. Sometimes your computer will even become super-slow and the MS Word document will start crashing every time you try to make a change after you've made several thousand corrections with the track changes feature turned on. Furthermore, authors don't always know how to view the document in their program or they might have a version of MS Word you don't have that will make how they view it different from how you see it. Occasionally, I will also return a PDF of the clean or edited copy so they can see the book the way I see it, although they still have to make their changes in the MS Word document. I've found most authors don't want to be bothered with all the changes in the edited version because it's overwhelming to them; they are happy just to use the clean copy to see what the text now says, and they are delighted by how smoothly it reads compared to the manuscript they initially sent me.

At this point, you may need to use your very best customer service skills because even though you explained what to do when making revisions, some clients just don't get it or they get confused. I have clients call me because they can't see the changes they're making in the manuscript. I ask a few questions to try to figure out why. It's not uncommon that they are looking at the file on their phone, which won't show the track changes. Then I have to tell them to go look at it on their computer when they get home. Some have various computer issues that I try to walk them through. Sometimes they call me because they accidentally turned off the track changes feature, so I walk them through how to turn it back on. Authors will have all kinds of computer issues, so you just have to be patient with them and help them as you can. If you don't know the answer, suggest they ask tech-savvy friends or family for help or they take their laptops to the nearest computer store for help. It's not your job to teach computer skills, but you will be asked computer questions regardless, so be prepared to help your clients as you can, and most importantly, remain patient or you will lose clients and all the clients they might have referred to you.

When authors send back manuscripts, be prepared to be amazed (preferable to frustrated) by how they messed up your beautifully edited book. Authors will put three spaces after words, put in two periods next to each other, run two words together, and, of course, leave typos in the manuscript, but that is why you have the track changes feature on—so you can see what they changed. I always page through and correct all the edits so I'm focusing only on the changes. Then, after I have corrected the changes, I accept them all and proofread the book. Sometimes, however, I'll send it back because the author has ignored or just not seen several of the suggestions I made. Again, a lot of patience is required.

You will find in this process that you end up doing a lot of little things you wouldn't have thought you'd have to do. I've had authors send me 2,000-word About the Author pages I've had to trim down to 500 words. I've had authors send me testimonials for their books from all their friends and family members and fellow authors that I've had to edit for them. Sometimes, I have written ten testimonials for authors to send out to people to sign because they didn't know what to write themselves. As I mentioned, I usually write the back cover descriptions for the books. These are all things that are really outside the job of an editor, but they are also things that make you an author's best friend.

In truth, it can be frustrating when authors can't collect their own testimonials, but if I'm working with first-time authors who don't know any other authors, I will often contact some of my former editing clients and ask them to write testimonials. It shouldn't take you more than an hour or two to do this, and the author will be extremely grateful for your help. (You should note here, too, that many of the testimonials on books are fake. Most people who write testimonials are happy to have the author or editor write the testimonial and then they just sign their names to them. Occasionally, some might ask to see the manuscript before giving a testimonial, but even these people will usually only read a chapter or just check to make sure the manuscript is well-written enough that it won't make them look bad if they endorse it. Fake testimonials are one of the dirty little secrets of the publishing industry, I'm afraid.)

Most editors don't look over layout proofs, but I always do because there are several opportunities during the layout process to introduce errors.

Authors don't know what to look for unless they've published several books. I never read the proofs because I've already proofread the book, but I've learned what kinds of errors to look for in the proofs. Chief among these are headers and page numbers. These are often found on blank pages where they don't belong, or if authors want chapter titles in the headers, there are bound to be errors for some chapters. Other formatting issues need to be looked for, such as an extra space between paragraphs, and typos in titles and sub-titles that were typed in, rather than pasted in, for whatever reason. Authors are grateful when you catch these errors. Sometimes authors also hire layout people who don't really know what they are doing. I've seen books laid out without page numbers, without headers, and even a book cover that didn't have the author's name on it. The author doesn't always know to look for these things, so again, you have to be the author's best friend in the process.

I always send my clients an email when the PDF of the book arrives instructing them how to make comments in the manuscript. Most of them have no idea that you can highlight or use sticky notes in a PDF, so I have to explain the process to them. Depending on whether they have Adobe Acrobat's latest version, or any version at all, they may have difficulty writing comments. In the case of the least tech-savvy, I tell them they can simply send me a list, and I will put in the sticky notes. Just a list doesn't really work for layout because when the layout person begins making changes in InDesign or Quark or whatever program is used, the text will shift. Telling layout to fix something on page 79 won't help if it shifted to page 78 or 81 because other changes moved that page. Here's a sample of the email I usually send to clients explaining how to mark up their proofs:

Dear Jane,

You'll want to look over the book and put in sticky notes anywhere you want a change. You can insert them by right clicking in the text where something needs to be fixed and then a sticky note option should come up. Click on that and a box will open for you to type the note in. You may also want to highlight words and then insert a comment with them. Highlighting is often easier because it's clear then what text you want to have changed, whereas sticky note placement is not always clear.

Please keep the notes as simple as possible. We don't need explanations for why you want to change something. Just say:

Add a line between these paragraphs

or

Change "that" to "than"

Simple commands that will be clear to Larry [the layout person] when he makes the changes.

When you finish putting in any corrections you find, send the file to me and then I will add anything I find to your corrections and also look over your corrections to make sure we don't introduce any typos. Then I'll send the file back to Larry. Once Larry makes the corrections, we'll go through and double-check them all to make sure nothing was missed.

If you can't open the file, you need to download Adobe Acrobat Reader to your computer. Go here to do so: https://get.adobe.com/reader/

If for some reason the sticky notes don't work for you, just send me a list that details the page, paragraph, and line where a change is needed. For example:

p. 73, 2nd paragraph, 3rd line, change "fat" to "fit"

Then I'll go through and put in the sticky notes. Again, we need to send Larry the changes in the PDF because once he starts changing the file, words move around. What was on a certain page will change in his master file, but not in the PDF where the notes are, so he'll still be able to find it.

If you have questions, just let me know.

Thanks,

Tyler

(Note, you may have to change the layout person's name as you send out this template, depending on how many different layout people you work with.)

Again, here is where you will need to be patient. Most authors make reasonable changes, but every once in a while, an author decides to rewrite the book at this stage. Before the book is laid out, you need to tell authors that once it's in layout, no changes are to be made except to fix typos or formatting issues. (This statement is in my editing agreement, but by this point in the process, most authors have forgotten about it.) Authors may well send you a few hundred "corrections" to sentences they want to reword anyway. When they put in sticky notes with their new sentences, they will likely introduce typos in those new sentences. You will need to proofread all the changes the author wants to make. Don't be afraid to inform authors they need to pay you extra if they do this and it takes up more of your time than you allotted in your original price quote for correcting of proofs.

Once layout makes the corrections, you'll also have to double-check them all. Most layout people will copy and paste text from the correction comment into the file, but some will type in the change if it's just a word or two; in this case, layout may potentially create typos as well. You need to be patient with both the author and the layout person, neither of whom likely have your editing skills. You also need to be sure you are getting paid for all the time you spend doing this. It usually isn't a super time-consuming process, which is why I just add an hour to my initial price quote to cover looking at the proofs, but if an author decides to rewrite the book, be upfront about the fact that you will have to charge extra for your time. If authors don't want to pay, let them know any typos introduced into the book during the layout and proofing process will not be your responsibility.

Most authors will be willing to pay extra for your time because they want their books to be perfect, but every once in a while, you will be dealing with an unreasonable author, so be pleasant but firm, and if need be, clarify how much time it will take (your best guess) so there are no surprises. You may want to charge hourly or give the author a price quote for extra corrections at this point, although guessing how much work it will be may be difficult. If you have a good layout person, you might find that 300 corrections are made almost perfectly and you only have to fix a few of them a second time, but I've also seen cases where five corrections have had to be fixed multiple times because the layout person wasn't clear on what needed to be done or was just a sloppy typist and kept introducing new errors. Again, patience is mandatory during this process.

In the end, you want to produce a high quality product, and you are working with the author and layout person to ensure that. You want authors to feel good about the process and be pleased with the results. Remember, happy clients return and/or refer.

In short, excellent customer service is a must if you want to stay in business.

Chapter 7
Yes, Yes, Yes—No

"When you say no to the wrong people, it opens up the space for the right
people to come in."

— Joe Calloway, *Magnetic: The Art of Attracting Business*

WHEN YOU FIRST start out editing, business may be slow or
almost nonexistent. Therefore, you don't want to start out by
turning people away, no matter how bad the job (unless it's truly
impossible or goes against your principles).

The beginning of your editing career is the time to say yes to everyone
who comes your way. Of course, not every job you take on will be easy, and
eventually, you may end up feeling overwhelmed. When you reach that point,
it's time to become more discerning about what you say yes to. Ultimately,
you want to be doing work you enjoy, not drudgery just for a paycheck. Most
of the work I say no to is work I know will end up being more work than the
author can pay for, or I know it just doesn't match my skill set and someone
else can probably do it better.

Following are some examples of jobs I would say no to now, although in
some cases, I said yes to them in the past.

Editing Daily Chapters or Blog Posts

One of the biggest problems with being a freelance editor is you don't
get a lot of repeat business, since most authors only write one book. Once
I finish editing an author's book and it is published, I may never hear from
that author again. This isn't necessarily a bad thing because authors, provided
they're happy with your work, may meet other aspiring authors and refer
them to you. You can hope this happens, but I doubt one-third of the authors
I do work for refer someone to me, so you can't count on this.

When you find an author who wants to work with you regularly and long-term, you can start to feel you have a little job security because you have a somewhat reliable source of income. That doesn't mean it's a lucrative source of income—most authors don't have large budgets—but a bird in the hand is better than two in the bush.

Even if authors only write one book, that doesn't mean they will never need your editing skills again. Serious authors get busy creating ways to market their books, and that includes writing various types of marketing materials. I can't tell you how I cringe when I see an author whose book I've edited writing posts on Facebook that are full of typos. When I see those posts, I know that most discerning readers would never want to read the author's book because they'll think it is as badly written as the Facebook posts. In other words, quite often authors need someone to protect them from themselves, especially the one-book authors who only wrote the book to further a speaking or business career and are not interested in learning how to be good writers.

If you need more work, one thing you can do is offer to continue working with authors by editing their daily or weekly blog posts, marketing pieces, email blasts, newsletters, etc. Most authors never even think about this need, so be sure to point it out to them. Few will take you up on it, but those who do will be happy to have your continued support just like you'll be happy to have more work.

I've agreed to edit blog posts for several authors over the years, and I still do so for a select few whose writing isn't too painful to edit and who will send me a blog post on a weekly or monthly basis. The nice thing about these customers is they provide a reliable source of income. It may only take a few minutes to do and you may only earn a few dollars from it, but it's consistent. I have authors who send me short, 500- to 1,000-word blog posts every week, and I charge them a $10 minimum fee, possibly more, depending on the length of each blog post. In these cases, I charge by the hour; for example, let's say you are charging $50 an hour. If you edit someone's blog post in 24 minutes, that's 40 percent of an hour, so I'd charge $20 for the job. I usually keep a running tab for the author, and then when we reach an agreed-upon dollar amount for payment, usually $100 or $200, I send the author a PayPal invoice.

The disadvantage with this kind of work is that you have to be available to edit the author's blog posts on the same day(s) each week (sometimes they will send it a day early—sometimes at the last minute). This can tie you down if you have other things to do, but if it's just one or a few blogs posts a week, it's not a big deal. You can also be protective of your time by letting the author know you need a twenty-four-hour turnaround time and also that you charge a $10 minimum, or whatever seems suitable to you, regardless of length.

Be aware, also, that most of the authors who will want you to edit blog posts for them will likely write five or six when their book first launches, and then they'll get too busy or bored to write more. Soon you won't have any more blog posts to edit from them. That's been the case with most authors I've worked with, but I have a few whose blog posts I've been editing for five years or more.

I think committing to editing something on a weekly basis is fine and allows you to remain fairly flexible. However, I would recommend staying away from any daily editing commitments because they will stress you out and play havoc with your schedule. For example, I had an author who wanted me to edit a chapter a day of her novel that she would then post online over the course of a month. Several problems arose from this situation. First of all, some of her chapters were short—500 or so words—but sometimes they were 5,000 words. I could edit the 500 words in ten or twenty minutes, but the longer chapters might take a couple of hours, which was a significant chunk of my day that I hadn't planned for. This was particularly problematic when the author often didn't send the chapters to me until 8 p.m. and she wanted them back as early as possible. Since she was in an earlier time zone, she didn't understand that it was difficult for me to promise same-day turnaround. Because I was doing the editing piecemeal, it was also hard for me to follow her novel's plot and I couldn't go back and fix things in earlier chapters to agree with changes she made later. In short, I would never recommend serializing anything unless the entire work was written and edited before the serialization began. Consequently, I felt I could not do high quality work for her and didn't really want my name associated with the product.

I had another client I edited and posted daily blog entries for who initially told me I would always have the blog by 10 a.m. and it had to be posted by 2 p.m. the same day. Every day at 10 a.m., I'd look in my email for the blog post to edit and post it; half the time, it wouldn't be there. I'd wait, send an email about noon, asking where it was, get a response about 2 p.m. saying it would be there in a few minutes, and then I'd get it about 5 or 6 p.m. and have to delay my dinner to edit it because the author always wanted it posted right away since it was already several hours late. This relationship didn't last long. Eventually, the author decided he couldn't afford to keep paying me daily for the editing. I was fine with that because I felt like I was on-call all day waiting for a blog post and constantly checking for it. It made it difficult for me to plan my day since I never knew when this blog post was coming. Had the author not decided to let me go, I would have likely ended the relationship soon after just because the meager amount of money I was getting was not worth the anxiety. Had the author consistently had the blog post to me at the same time or earlier every day, the relationship would have been beneficial for both of us and could have continued for years.

A situation like this last one is all the more reason to charge a minimum per blog post or even have a daily retainer fee so you get paid regardless of whether the author sends you work that day. That way you will cover the time you spend constantly checking your email and be somewhat compensated for your anxiety.

Ghost Writing

A lot of authors will also ask about ghostwriting. I have always refused to ghostwrite a book. However, you may choose otherwise, especially since ghostwriting can be a very lucrative job. Most ghostwriters make about as much as editors per hour, although I know of some who make as much as $125 an hour. You will also be paid for a lot more hours as a ghostwriter than as an editor. Starting out, if you are asked to ghostwrite, you may want to do so if you need the money or the idea of ghostwriting appeals to you. Just remember it is a very time-consuming job. Because I've had a steady stream of editing clients, and I can usually do a full edit of a book in three to five days, I have always said no to ghostwriting. I know a ghostwriting project could take weeks or months and I would have to turn away editing work or put authors on a lengthy waiting list. In addition, while I find writing my own books fun and energizing, being forced to write on a topic I'm not interested in and that I may only have minimal knowledge about is too energy-sapping for me. I might enjoy editing a business book, but writing one is not something I'm interested in, no matter what I'm getting paid. I would rather expend that energy in writing my own books.

That said, at times, I have agreed to ghostwrite smaller pieces such as blog posts, essays, and articles. I have only done this for a few clients whose topics I was interested in and knowledgeable enough about that I could do a good job at it. I would never agree to ghostwrite for a chemistry blog, but I might say yes to writing a weekly article on book marketing ideas. In these situations, I've charged the author hourly or we agreed on a set price per article or blog post I wrote. For example, I used to ghostwrite a blog for an author who wanted three posts a week, each about 500 words. We agreed on a price for those three blog posts, I was free to write on whatever topic in the subject area I wanted, and she paid me weekly for the work I did. Other authors have wanted me to ghostwrite articles on very specific topics. They would tell me the topic and maybe some bullet points they wanted to cover, and then I would charge them hourly because sometimes it would be a 500-word blog post and sometimes, a 2,500-word magazine article, so it just made more sense to charge hourly.

Again, ghostwriting such pieces on a regular basis can provide a steady income, even if you're only getting $40 a week for the one article you write. Regardless, that's money you can count on, and it will feed you for a couple of days. It's not worth it, however, if you are not happy doing it, you have to expend too much energy on it, or you are tied down to a rigid daily schedule. For the author I would write three blog posts a week for, I would usually write all three on Monday and deliver them on Friday. By not sending them until Friday, it gave me wiggle room if I was sick on Monday or had another project I had to get done. Of course, you always want to wow your customers by delivering things early, but in this situation, I quickly learned that if I delivered the blog posts on Monday or Tuesday, the author came to expect that every week and then complained if I didn't deliver them that day, so I eventually built an expectation that she would have them every Friday and I never varied from it.

Of course, every client and situation will be different. You may end up saying yes to something you wish you had said no to. In those cases, stick it out for a little while to see whether the situation improves, and if not, respectfully let the author know you want to end the work relationship. It's also great if you can refer these authors to someone else so you don't leave them hanging, or at the very least, give them notice a couple of weeks in advance so they have time to find someone else to do the work. Bottom line, it's never worth it to do something that will make you miserable.

Toxic Book Topics

Most of the authors I edit books for have something worthwhile to say. They may not be the best communicators, but their ideas are good and they just need me to help them get their messages out into the world in presentable formats. I would say that has been the case with 99 percent of the authors I've worked with. Yes, some of them will write better books than others, and I often find that the self-help book I'm editing doesn't say anything I haven't heard before, but I also realize that if it's the first self-help book someone reads, it will be valuable to that reader.

However, there are always exceptions. You may occasionally have to turn away authors because their book topics are just not something you want to deal with. There is always a tactful way to do this without hurting the author's feelings. It isn't always easy to say no, but it's easier than taking on a project you know will only bring you angst.

For example, I once turned away an author because her book's premise was that school shootings were happening because Satan was possessing our children; the book was supposed to help the reader determine whether students were possessed by Satan, and if not, how to protect students from becoming possessed. This topic was the last thing I needed—it was depressing and, in my opinion, far-fetched. I've edited lots of Christian, spiritual, and religious books, but sometimes I find that the author's religious views are just too far from mine. Some editors might see such a book as a great opportunity to play devil's advocate with authors and help them come up with opposing arguments to answer. I have done that with some authors, especially when there are only portions of their arguments I disagree with. However, while I am open-minded and do not deny that anything is possible, this topic was so revolting and depressing to me that I just wasn't up to spending hours every day thinking about it. I also thought the book was too far beyond what most theologians would see as reasonable. Therefore, I politely told the author I didn't feel I was qualified to edit the book. I told her Christian books were not my specialty and referred her to a Christian book editing service.

I turned away another author who sent me a sex manual to edit. Again, I'm an open-minded person, but this book had photos of sexual positions and details about achieving orgasm. Even that didn't bother me as much as the fact that it was very badly written. Ultimately, I discovered that all the photos had been taken off internet sites and were not the author's property. Worse, most of the text had been copied off the internet too. I could have edited this book by basically rewriting all of the content so that nothing copyrighted remained in the book, but I told the author it would be a ton of work and cost him a lot of money; furthermore, if he published the book as it was, he would be violating copyright laws and also angering readers who had paid for something they could have gotten for free on the internet. Wisely, the author decided it wasn't worth continuing the book project.

I reserve the right to turn away any books that are racist, sexist, pornographic, filled with hate speech, or in any way do a disservice to society. I am sure there are editors out there who will take on these kinds of books, but I don't need to expend my time and energy on them. I prefer to use my skills to make the world a better place.

I have gotten some political and religious or spiritual books where I've disagreed with the author but just kept my mouth shut and done the work, or I've played devil's advocate so the author will see where parts of the arguments are weak and can be prepared for any opposition readers might feel. As I mentioned earlier, I've edited several books by authors who claim they are channeling God or some other entity or historical personage. I even have friends who are channels and mediums whom I believe are at least well-meaning, and in some cases, have surprised me with knowledge and messages that lead me to believe they really are able to connect with some Higher Power, so I remain open-minded on such topics.

Sometimes, you can also help an author who means well but may have views that will only be offensive to readers. For example, I once edited a religious book in which the author made a passing negative reference to homosexuality. I convinced her to remove it because she would probably infuriate half her readers with the comment and it was not a central point in her book. I reminded her that even Christians are divided on this issue. Other times, authors have inadvertently made sexist or racist statements in their books that they didn't realize would be offensive. In these cases, I've helped them remove or reword the offensive passages. As an editor, I try to respond as I believe the intended reader will, so if I think most readers will be offended by something, I feel it's my job to let authors know certain passages or arguments they are making could be issues. If authors choose to ignore my advice, that is their prerogative, but at least I have done my job. If an author is nasty to me in response, then I will finish the job and remain professional, but I will think twice before agreeing to edit that author's next book.

These situations, of course, are few and far between. I can count on one hand the number of times I've turned away an author because of an offensive book topic. That said, sometimes you're well into a project before you realize it is offensive. In most of these cases, the authors aren't always intending to offend and you can play devil's advocate to help them see the problems with their positions. I feel it's always important to point out these issues because that way, when readers give books one-star reviews at Amazon, the authors can't come back to me complaining that I didn't do my job by warning them about potentially volatile issues in their books.

Subject Matter You're Not Knowledgeable About

Occasionally, an author sends me a book I simply don't feel qualified to edit. These are few and far between. With most topics, I can find answers online if I don't understand something in the book, or I can just ask the author to explain some concept to me so I can rewrite it in lay terms for the reader. At times, however, I have told authors upfront that their topics aren't ones I feel qualified to help with, and then I let them know if they want me to do the job, I will, but they have to keep in mind that I am no expert on the subject. Some authors want to work with me anyway; others I refer to another editor whom I think will be better qualified.

Below are the few genres and subject matters I may decide not to edit and why.

Science Fiction: For a long time, I was not a fan or a reader of science fiction, so I didn't feel qualified to judge whether these books were good or not. There are certain tropes in the genre that are accepted that I didn't understand or was unsure about, such as how much explanation you have to give about certain technologies and what you can just assume readers know, so I told authors it would be best to find someone more familiar with current science fiction and what sells to edit their books. In a couple of cases, I had authors look for another editor, then come back to me, still wanting me to edit their books, so then I agreed. As time went by, I became more interested in science fiction and now I enjoy editing science fiction books and don't turn them away.

Children's Books: I don't have children and can't pretend to know what children today like. It's also true that some children's authors write and publish their books without even letting a child read it and give them feedback beforehand. I always tell children's book authors to visit a classroom to read their books to and get feedback from children. I also refer them to another editor who specializes in children's books.

Poetry: I am rarely asked to edit poetry, but I will usually agree to look at it and then decide. If they are simple, rhyming poems, I will often agree to edit them to help with the meter and rhyme, but I usually refuse to edit most other poetry since punctuation, capitalization, etc. is all subjective in poetry, especially in free verse. Honestly, I just don't get most modern poetry. I prefer classic poets like Tennyson, Wordsworth, Eliot, and Frost. I'm not the editor for someone who wants to write twenty-first-century free verse.

Cookbooks: I don't cook—unless spaghetti and scrambled eggs count—so if I'm editing a cookbook and authors say to use 3 tablespoons of something when they really mean 3 teaspoons, I'm not going to catch that. Better that someone who actually cooks proofread the cookbook.

You may find that you don't like to edit novels or business books or science books, etc. Most editors have their areas of specialty—mine are usually self-help, business books, and novels. Focus on your strengths and edit books that fit what you're comfortable with. Find some fellow editors who have different strengths and weaknesses; then refer authors to them for topics you don't feel comfortable editing and ask the editors to return the favor. Then you won't be just turning away work; you'll be building a relationship with another editor who might refer work to you.

Conclusion

When you first start out, you will likely be willing to say yes to almost everything just to pay your bills. Over time, though, when you're no longer living from one job to the next but can build up your bank account and also your workload, you'll be able to say no to situations that you know just are not right for you. Don't feel guilty in these situations. It's not always easy to say no, but a few hours of discomfort for doing so is far easier than dealing with a situation for weeks or months that will make you miserable. Say no when you need to and be available to say yes when better opportunities come your way.

There is one final situation in which you may want to say no, and that's when you have to deal with nasty or clueless authors. This topic deserves an entire chapter of its own, so we'll talk about it more in Chapter 11.

Chapter 8
Juggling 101

"I tend to take on a lot of things. And then they all just seem to happen at once. Or maybe I'm not good at saying 'No.' But the juggling's fun."

— Joel Edgerton

ONCE YOUR BUSINESS starts to take off, you may find yourself feeling overwhelmed. The strategy to use here is to remember, first off, that you are editing books, not performing life-or-death surgery. No book is so urgent it can't wait a week or two if need be. Also, while a client may be thrilled that you can start editing a book right away, you need to train authors about what to expect. If you explain that you are backed up or very busy at the moment, but you can start on a certain date, most authors will understand. Here are a few strategies for getting everything done as efficiently as possible. By adopting these strategies, I have yet to have a client complain I took too long or didn't meet the deadline I initially promised.

Underpromise and Overdeliver

When I take on a book project, I always tell the client I will need at least two weeks to do the two initial edits as described in my editing agreement. Now, some authors will send you a short manuscript that is 20,000 words that you know you can turn around in two or three days, but it's best to say two weeks anyway because you never know what might happen—whether it's a family emergency of your own or having to rescue another author who has a crisis. If need be, tell the author three weeks, depending on the book and how busy and how fast you are. Frankly, even four or six weeks is not unreasonable. The thing is always to return the manuscript to the author on or before the date promised.

That said, if you're really busy, you might also want to delay returning a book even though you've finished it. Here's why: Let's say I may have a 50,000-word book I've spent two weeks editing. During those two weeks, another 50,000-word book has come in that I plan to start on next. I send the first book back to the author and start on the second book. The first author returns the manuscript with corrections the next day (sometimes even within a few hours; some authors think they get gold stars for speed-reading. They don't.). I decide I better proofread the corrections right away rather than make the author wait two more weeks to get the book to the printer. That said, if I put that book at the front of the line, it pushes the second author's book back a couple of days. Imagine if you already had three books in your queue after the first author's book. This is why I constantly tell authors it will take longer than I know it will take—so I can get the second book mostly edited before I even return the first book—that way I don't have to delay the second author and the first author still gets the book back within the expected time frame.

Furthermore, sometimes after editing a book, I want a few days to mull it over before I write up my suggestions for improvements. Better to mull something over rather than hastily send it off without thought. As the old proverb says, "If a thing is worth doing, it's worth doing well."

The speed-reader author is a rare breed, so that situation won't happen often. More likely, an author will take a week or even a month to return a book to you. I've had some authors take a year or more. In any case, you're always guessing on the most likely scenario for when a book will come back to you, and you have no control over when that will be. Plan accordingly by giving yourself time cushions; that way you keep everyone satisfied and put as little pressure on yourself as possible.

Another advantage in delaying sending back manuscripts is that you need distance from a book. If you edit a book on Monday and return it to the author, and then the author returns it to you Tuesday morning, expecting you to proofread it right away, you will be less likely to catch errors because you're so familiar with the material. If a few weeks go by while the author is doing revisions and you're working on other books, you're more likely to catch errors when you proofread it. Even if you can just delay sending the book back for a couple of days, you can get enough distance from it to make a difference.

Juggling also often requires you to work on more than one book at a time. It is not at all uncommon for me to work on three or four books within the same week. Sometimes I will have a long novel of 100,000 words that I told the author I would return in three weeks' time. I then will edit 10,000 words of that book every day, which might take me about three hours or all of my morning basically, but as long as I meet my goal each day, I can then proofread the other three manuscripts I got on the same day throughout that week or next. I can usually proofread about 10,000 words an hour, so I might be able to proofread three books in a week and still get a lot done on the long novel if the books I have to proofread are relatively short, such as 40,000 words each.

Planning Your Day and Week

I usually have my day and my entire week planned out in advance. Granted, sometimes a book will take more or less time than I expect, and sometimes circumstances beyond my control will arise that will throw off my schedule, but by setting reasonable goals for myself each day, I am able to accomplish my tasks in a timely matter. I typically work an eight- or nine-hour day. In that time, I expect to get five hours of editing done on the primary book I'm working on. The rest of that time is taken up with answering email and doing smaller projects (editing a blog post, looking over proofs of a laid-out book, answering author phone calls, etc.) If it's a slow email day (rare, but it happens), I might get six or seven hours of editing done. If it's a crazy, busy day of email and phone calls, I still usually make my editing quota because I set a reasonable schedule for myself, and if need be, I can let some of the smaller tasks wait so I can get the bigger task done.

I'm not one to write down my tasks for the week, although I will occasionally make a list of everything I need to do. I will also sometimes leave what I need to do in my email inbox and then move it out when it's done; that way, I don't forget to do something. You may want to spend time on Friday afternoon or first thing Monday morning making a plan for the week. Monday is usually the better choice because projects may come in over the weekend.

You may also find that you need to rearrange things as they come in. Some authors will have strict deadlines because they might have a book release party or speaking engagement planned. I always try to put those authors at the front of the line to ensure they get their books finished on time. After all, I know if I had a book release party planned and no books for it, I wouldn't be happy. That said, don't force yourself to burn the candle at both ends for someone's unrealistic schedule. I've had authors call me on September 1 and say they need a book in print for an October 3 event. It is possible I could edit the book in a week, the layout person could lay it out in a week, and the printer could get it printed in two weeks, but that's a lot of stress for everyone, especially when you are probably already working with three or four other authors. If you have to turn the person away, go ahead. You already have enough work at this point anyway.

I've found that the people with these unrealistic expectations are the ones I'll work my butt off to get their book to, only to email it to them, not get a response from them for three days, and then have them tell me they are moving that month so they won't have time to work on the book until after October 1. I guess there's no scheduled book event in their near future after all, and I didn't even charge them anything extra for the added stress they gave me. (It's never a bad idea to charge more for a rush job.)

More Than Expected

Sometimes, authors will send back massive revisions beyond what is reasonable. In other words, they completely rewrite the book, filling it with the kinds of typos and grammar errors you already spent twenty hours fixing. If an author does this, you have a clause in your contract stating that revisions above 5,000 words (or whatever number you feel comfortable with) will cost extra. Let the author know right away that you are invoking that clause and will charge hourly. Make sure the author agrees to this before you do any additional work.

When an author rewrites the book to this extreme, it can also seriously mess up your schedule. Here's why: Most authors who return manuscripts to me have rewritten words and sentences throughout the manuscript. I expect to spend one or two hours editing those revisions. To do so, I page through the manuscript, look for the track changes markings, and fix all the new errors that have been introduced. Then, given that it's a 50,000-word book, I expect I'll spend about five hours proofreading it. Once the author returns the manuscript to me, I'm expecting it to be about seven hours of work—probably 1.5 days' worth. When an author sends back a book with almost every sentence rewritten, it might take ten hours just to go through and edit all the changes, depending on the quality of the author's writing. Furthermore, because of the number of changes, I'm likely to miss more errors than usual. This means more work and time spent proofreading the book. In that case, what should have been a five-hour proofread might take seven hours. Now I have seventeen hours of work to do when I planned on seven. That's at least two extra days of work.

If this happens, you need to let the author know upfront that you will need extra time to make the corrections and that you are invoking the clause stating you charge for excessive revisions. In this case, a vague statement like, "I should have it back to you next week," is usually sufficient, since next week could mean three or eleven days depending on what day of the week it currently is.

Being an editor is always a juggling act, but as time goes by, you'll get better at juggling, and you'll also likely become faster because you're more knowledgeable and have learned tricks that make your life easier. For example, you'll come to remember that "backseat" is one word and not have to look it up each time you see it, and you'll learn to search for and replace recurring errors or do mass changes to save yourself time.

Being an editor and juggling all of these books can be stressful, but from the start of this book, I've made it clear this is not a dream job. However, if you get this busy, just remember to be grateful that you have plenty of work. Worst-case scenario, you may occasionally have to turn a client away or lose a prospective client who doesn't want to wait.

When you reach this point, you may also decide it's time to hire/contract with another editor to lessen your workload. I'll talk more about how to do that in Chapter 15. But first, it's time to talk about how to keep your business afloat while enjoying the nomad lifestyle. Then I'll share some stories of successes and give you a few tips on how to deal with cannibal clients. Hopefully, the next few chapters will give you some insights into what you should prepare for in your editing career so you can keep your business prospering while not wearing yourself out.

Chapter 9
Living the Nomad Life:
Traveling and Taking Time Off

"Life might be difficult for a while, but I would tough it out because living in a foreign country is one of those things that everyone should try at least once. My understanding was that it completed a person, sanding down the rough provincial edges and transforming you into a citizen of the world."

— David Sedaris

I N MY OPINION, the hardest part of being a nomad editor is the nomad part. I say that because I am a recovering workaholic. However, I've learned that a strong sense of boundaries—with clients and even with yourself—will allow you to make being an editor the best possible job for you. That means not only enjoying your work, but traveling, living abroad, or just taking time off when you need or want to.

I won't lie. Being self-employed, especially in the beginning, makes it difficult to take time off. You have too many responsibilities and wear too many hats: not just editor, but customer service representative, accountant, debt collector, marketer, janitor, etc. Perhaps hardest of all, you need to be human resources—you don't need to track your vacation days since you can have as many as you want, but you do need to make sure you take vacations. As a self-employed editor, you need to work just as hard at protecting your free time as you do at taking care of your clients.

I am the first to admit I do not take off as much time as I should or would like to. Primarily, that is because I always have one book after another coming in to edit; plus, I never know when the next book will come in or when an author will return a book to me for a second edit. Somehow, I have always managed to keep a steady flow of books going back and forth between me and authors so that I rarely am left without something to do. Occasionally, I do find I have two or three days where I don't have much work, but I know at any minute work can come in unexpectedly. Often, I'll finish a project on Monday, not have anything to do on Tuesday morning, and by Tuesday afternoon, have enough work to keep me busy for weeks to come. Because of this unpredictability about when you'll have work, you need to set boundaries with yourself and your clients so you are successful at taking time off.

Setting Boundaries

In the beginning, you will be eager for work, and you may even be willing to cancel plans to do work to please your clients. In time, though, as you build up your business, you'll be less willing to sacrifice your free time. If you plan to take your family to Disney World the first week of September, but two days before your trip, someone sends you a book that needs to be at the printer by the end of the month, and you know the only way you can pull that off is to cancel your vacation, by all means, tell the client *no*. Otherwise, you will end up resenting the client, and your family will end up resenting you.

As a general rule, never put your work before your family or other relationships, especially when it comes to breaking plans. If your daughter, just out of the blue, wants you to play with her when you're working to finish a project the client needs that day that you agreed to deliver on time, that's a little different, but if you have personal commitments scheduled, don't change them.

If someone in Hawaii calls you in New York at 5 p.m. your time (11 a.m. in Hawaii) and wants you to edit an article and return it that day, and it means missing going out to dinner with your friends, that's a bit harder. Missing dinner will likely not kill you or your friends, unless you've cancelled dinner for the same reason multiple times and your friends are becoming irritated. However, any reasonable person in Hawaii will realize that people in New York are six hours ahead (or five depending on the time of year). In such a situation, consider your relationship with the author—is this person a lucrative client you've done work for before, or is it someone new? Consider that if this article will only take an hour of your time, you can edit it after dinner, or postpone dinner if it will not inconvenience your friends too much. Use your best judgment in such situations, but also remember that if you train your clients to respect your boundaries, you won't end up in this scenario very often. They will learn that you need twenty-four to forty-eight hours to turn a job around.

Early in my editing career, it seemed like I was always doing stuff that was an "emergency" for an author (e.g., editing a document for a workshop the author sent me the morning of the workshop). The truth is, there is no such thing as an emergency in the editing and publishing world. If people do not plan far enough in advance to have what they need for their events, that is not your fault. You can be kind and do the work at the last minute if you don't mind, but don't feel obligated. If you must say no, kindly explain you have other commitments and that you're sorry you can't help.

Remember, books are not brain surgery. Books are amazing, life-changing products, but if a book has to wait an extra day, week, or month, no one is going to die.

As hard as it is, learn to set boundaries. Truthfully, I found that as soon as I started to set boundaries, the Law of Attraction quit sending me authors with emergencies. I quit sending out the crisis mode, "I'm available to you 24/7 for whatever needs to be done, you poor planning, high maintenance, last minute author, you" vibe, and the Universe quit matching me with such authors.

That said, I know setting boundaries is not easy, especially in the beginning, but as you practice setting them, you will get better at it. Here are a few tips to get you started:

- **Quit answering the phone after office hours.** If you don't answer, clients can't beg you for help. They might leave you messages, but they know you may not get their voicemails in time to relieve their emergencies. Of course, after you listen to their messages, you can decide whether you want to call them back. Sometimes, I will call back after hours because my schedule for the next day is already full, or I will call back if it is a simple issue that will only take a minute of my time. But if I have other things to do, even if it's just relaxing, I will wait until the next day.

- **State your office hours on your voicemail.** By stating your office hours, you set clients' expectations for when you may call them back. Those clients will also know going forward that they won't be able to reach you if they call outside those hours.

- **Email instead of calling back.** Many clients will send an email within a few minutes of calling you. Whenever possible, I respond via email rather than calling them. I will also email if clients tell me what they need in the voicemail. Email is faster. For example, if I get a quick grammar question, I'll email the answer back with an example. Then clients have a visual so there's no confusion, since something like how to punctuate a sentence properly might get confusing if discussed over the phone. Sending an email also avoids further questions on the phone. That's not to say you shouldn't try to be unbelievably helpful—but if it's Sunday afternoon and you have friends coming over in ten minutes to watch the game, a quick email will be better than a phone call.

- **Tell people the best way to communicate with you.** We all prefer to communicate in different ways, but we also need to understand our clients also have their own preferences. Personally, I dislike texting because I have big, klutzy fingers so it takes me a long time to write a text without typos in it; therefore, I tell clients the best way to communicate with me is through email. Some will still prefer to call me, which is fine. Some will also initially text me to make contact. I'll text them back to give them my email address but then generally communicate only through email. If you prefer texting over email or talking on the phone over texting, do what works for you but also take into consideration what your clients prefer.

- **Set expectations upfront.** When you agree to edit a book, let the author know upfront when to expect to hear from you. I usually tell clients it will take two or three weeks and that I will contact them if I have questions or give them an update in a week. I then do ask questions or give updates so the client isn't emailing me every day to ask if I'm done yet. The same is true when clients email me questions or a file that needs to be looked at. If I can't respond at that moment with an answer or turn the work around right after getting the email, I will tell the client, "I'll get back to you tomorrow," or "Give me a couple of days and I'll return this to you."

- **Always reply.** Clients expect immediate responses. If they send you an email or text, reply as quickly as you can, within reason. A simple, "Got it. Thanks," will remove the author's anxiety. If you don't reply in a timely manner, the author may keep trying to contact you until you do. Set your clients' minds at ease as quickly as possible; you will be setting your own mind at ease as a result. That said, be reasonable; you will have anxious clients and then you will have laid-back ones. You'll get to know which is which and what each will expect from you and can respond accordingly.

- **Communicate time off with clients beforehand.** Once you've set the above boundaries, let clients know when you'll be unavailable. I usually tell clients a couple of weeks in advance when I'm going to be on vacation, and I remind them a couple of times after that if I'm in the middle of working on a project with them. I'll also notify clients in my newsletter that I send out every month or two so they'll know I'll be away. That doesn't mean you have to tell clients you won't be around two hours on Friday because you are going to lunch with a friend, but if you're going to be out the entire day or week, let them know.

- **Have autoresponders in place when you are away.** Send an out of office automatic reply to clients' emails when you are going to be out of the office for an extended period. In it, state which days you will be away and when you will respond to emails. For example, "I will be on vacation March 7-12. I will return all messages the week of March 13." Do the same with your outgoing voicemail message. These messages don't mean you can't reply to emails or phone calls during your time away, but they set clients' expectations. Also, note that I said I would return calls "the week of" and not on the first day I'm back. That is because I might have more calls to return than I can manage in a day, especially if I'm exhausted from travel. It's also very likely—this has happened to me more times than I can count—that your flight is delayed and you end up getting home a day later than expected, so that message gives you a bit of a buffer zone. Once you go on vacation and your clients realize you truly are gone, after a day or two, they'll quit calling or emailing, so you really won't be bombarded with the usual number of emails you get each day. People will get sick of your autoresponder message and quit emailing you, or they will simply get the message you are unavailable and wait for your response. Respond with care if you do respond while you are away—if you act like you have no autoresponder on and reply immediately, clients will get the idea you're available and keep emailing you. An email from you is always an invitation to write you back.

- **Make a promise to yourself that you will abide by the boundaries you set.** If you're like me, you'll find it easier to train clients than to train yourself. I'll admit it; at times, I get an adrenaline rush from being constantly busy, and when I take a day off, I miss it—I'm addicted to it. I can't tell you how many times I have found myself checking email on weekends or holidays only to feel disappointed there's no client request for help. I'll click the "Get Messages" button multiple times just to be sure. If you find yourself doing this, you have a problem, and it's a sign you need to get a life. Promise yourself you will limit your email time to one hour each morning and each night, or half an hour, or just to fifteen-minute increments before each meal on the days you will not be working. If you're spending time with family or friends, let them know you need to take some time each day to check your email. They can help you figure out the best time to do that. If you are a workaholic, also ask them to help keep you off the computer; have them hold you to your promise to relax and enjoy their company—and not to spend the whole time with clients. Your most important relationships—including your relationship with yourself—will be far better as a result.

I make light of being a workaholic, but it is a real problem. If you need additional help, look for a local Workaholics Anonymous meeting at www.workaholics-anonymous.org. Both phone and in-person meetings are available, depending on your location. If you believe you are too busy to go to a meeting, then you definitely need one.

Keeping Your Business Afloat While You Are Away

If you are self-employed, it can be very difficult to take time off. You want to go on vacation, but you don't want to come home to twenty phone calls and five hundred emails, or worse, messages from prospects who decided to hire someone else because you weren't available. Here are three options for handling this situation so you won't dread returning from vacation or find you no longer have a business.

Option 1: Take Your Work With You. This solution is not the best one, but it may be the only one available to you when you first get started. Fortunately, we live in the age of cellphones, tablets, and laptops so it's easy to take your work with you wherever you go. On the flip side, unfortunately, we live in the age of cellphones, tablets, and laptops so it's easy to take your work with you wherever you go.

Technology is both the best friend and worst enemy of nomad editors. Case in point, look at the illustrations in this book. Yes, they are fun and convey the message that you can do editing from anywhere you want, but in each picture, the editor is intensely working away rather than looking at the scenery. Don't be that editor. If you learn to set boundaries as I recommended above, you can just work as needed without missing your vacation.

For example, let's say you're taking a bus tour of the British Isles for three weeks. You'll likely be staying in hotels that have Wi-Fi, so bring your laptop with you, and in the morning or evening or both, check your email. Do not plan to do any work during your vacation unless it's work that only takes you half an hour or less. For example, you might be willing to edit a client's 500-word blog post if you get it before you go down to breakfast, but don't plan to edit any books.

You don't want to be touring all day and then returning to the hotel at night so you can work five hours. It's supposed to be your vacation. You only want to do the bare minimum necessary to keep your business afloat and make sure a client with an urgent situation—needs to order a second edition of a book by Friday but wants you to double-check three corrections before the book goes to print—gets taken care of, and so prospective clients won't think you are ignoring them and go elsewhere.

As I said above, set a limit on how much time you'll spend checking email each day and stick to it. You can also choose not to respond for a few days to non-urgent emails, provided you have an outgoing message saying you're away—set up such a message even if you plan to check your email while you're gone. Once you get in vacation mode, you may decide you don't want to check your email every day after all. Remember, you are only checking your email during your vacation to ensure your sanity by not having 500 emails to respond to when you get home. There is no need to do anything beyond that. If you tell clients you are on vacation when you respond to them and let them know when you will be able to get to their projects, the vast majority will understand and wait. If they don't understand, you don't want to work with them anyway.

Option 2: Find someone you trust to be your customer service while you're away. At times when I've gone away, I've taken my laptop with me and responded to clients as needed, especially if I'm traveling within the United States and just going to visit friends. My friends all understand I need an hour or two to keep up with my work. Again, I have not edited books during these vacations. At other times, I've wanted a true vacation so I've had Larry answer my emails for me; this is particularly the case if I am traveling overseas, since you never know what to expect when you travel.

That said, even if you don't have an issue taking your work with you on vacation, I still recommend finding someone to monitor your email when you are away simply because emergencies happen. Here's a case in

point: In April 2017, I had no idea I would be taking a six-day vacation…
to the hospital. My appendix ruptured and next thing I knew, I was in a
hospital bed. I was in so much pain, both before and after the surgery,
that I couldn't have even sat up to work on a laptop. For a couple of days
over a weekend, I managed to respond to emails using my phone. I had
an IV in my left arm so I couldn't move my arm. All I could do was
lie on my back, hold my phone with my right hand, and type with my
thumb. That worked for a weekend, but by Sunday afternoon, I knew
there was no way I could handle the volume of email I would receive on
Monday—typing with my thumb. Plus I was exhausted and needed to
sleep and heal, so I called Larry and he went to my house, got my laptop,
and replied to my emails for me until I was home and able to go back to
work. If Larry hadn't been able to step in and give me peace of mind, I
would have never gotten any rest or recovered as quickly because I would
have been frantically trying to reply to clients on my phone or I would
have been worrying about all the emails not answered and the clients
who might be mad I wasn't responding.

If you don't have a Larry available to you (it needs to be someone
who knows something about your business; don't trust your mom or
even your spouse to do this; much as you love them, you don't want them
proofreading a client's back cover and saying it's good to go to the printer
when there are three typos on it), consider getting a virtual assistant you
can train before you go anywhere. Of course, hiring a virtual assistant
overseas will be most cost-effective, but if you go this route, make certain
the person has impeccable English. Someone who can't write a complete
sentence will send your clients running because they expect you and all
your staff, since you're an editor, to write perfect English.

If you don't want a virtual assistant, I suggest finding someone local,
perhaps through a temporary service like Manpower, whom you can
train, or you can simply advertise or find a student intern from your local
college's English department. Find someone you are compatible with and
can trust. Then you'll be able to sleep at night knowing your business is
in competent hands.

Option 3: Do a hybrid of the above options. Personally, I think a
hybrid of the first two options is your best solution. Begin by setting up a
separate email account you don't give out to anyone except your assistant.
Let your assistant check the regular email account you normally check
every day. The assistant can delete all the spam emails and send out

responses to clients that say things like "Got it. I'll make sure Tyler has it when he gets back from vacation," or "Yes, Tyler does both proofreading and editing." The assistant can also forward to your private email account any emails that absolutely need your attention. Then, rather than fifty emails a day to read, you may only have a couple.

You can also reply directly to your assistant, who will then reply to the client for you so you don't end up having a long email discussion with your client. If possible, you can also just have a short daily or weekly call with your assistant to handle any issues that need handling. These calls could be done by phone or by Skype if you are overseas. If you plan to use your cellphone, check with your provider about roaming charges and whether you need to add an international service to your phone package. You might also try picking up a local throwaway phone, although make sure you get one with directions in English so you don't have problems learning how to use it. Often, phone cards can also be purchased that are relatively inexpensive. Trust me, you don't want to be making long distance calls from your hotel room. I did that once in Turkey. An eight-minute call to my mom cost me $64.00. Of course, another problem with phone calls is that the difference in time zones and your perhaps unpredictable travel schedule may make it difficult to have a regularly scheduled call. However, some situations may require a phone call if the matter is too cumbersome to explain over email. Do whatever works for you so you won't worry about work when you're away from it.

Travel Tips

If you are going to be traveling, remember the possibility always exists that something can be lost or stolen. You could also experience damaged equipment. If you bring a laptop with you, keep it in your possession at all times while in airports. Do not put it in a suitcase since you never know when luggage might get lost, damaged, or stolen. Here are a few other tips for protecting your business while traveling.

- **Buy a travel adapter and a surge protector.** Almost every country uses different-shaped electrical connections and even different voltage, so you may need to purchase a travel adapter. That said, your computer might already be prepared to deal with these differences. For example, I know an author who lugged adapters with her to the United Kingdom only to be told by Apple that her iPad was already set up to use either, so you may want to double-check what your own equipment can do before you buy something you don't need. If you do need an adapter, you can often buy one that should work for an entire region, like Europe, but it doesn't hurt to buy one specific to the country you're traveling to. You absolutely want to protect your electronics if you are working abroad, so buy a surge protector also. Plug your laptop or other device into the surge protector. Then plug the surge protector into the converter to ensure your protection.

- **Use a flashdrive for backup.** Every day I back up my work on a flashdrive. I use the program FreeFileSync, which Larry installed on my computer (he's also my IT guy), to update my documents so only the newest files from my computer get moved to the flashdrive. This process usually takes about two minutes each day and is worth it in case my computer crashes or a document becomes damaged. Then I can always find the document on my flashdrive and put it back on my computer. Sure, I might have lost a few hours' work, but that's better than losing all of it. I recommend you put your flashdrive on your keychain or in your pocket so it is always with you—just be careful not to let it fall out of your pocket.

- **Save your documents in the cloud.** Saving documents to the cloud is basically the same as backing them up on a flashdrive except that they will be available to you anywhere you have internet access and they can't be lost in a fire. The simplest way is to email documents to yourself so they are in your inbox on a server. You can also use a service like Dropbox where you upload them to your own personal folder or a shared folder. The advantage to the cloud is that you are not likely to lose documents like you would if you lost a flashdrive. Also, don't forget that a flashdrive could get damaged and then be unusable. Of course, your laptop could also get damaged. If both your laptop and flashdrive get damaged (e.g., your soon-to-be-ex gets sick of your workaholic ways and throws them in the lake), you're out of luck if you didn't save to the cloud.

- **Keep all electronics fully charged.** Make sure while traveling that you nightly charge your phone and you keep your laptop plugged in while working on it. That way, if you find yourself in a situation where perhaps your laptop or phone charger's cord becomes damaged or you need to make a phone call or check email on your phone because your laptop completely died, you will have several hours of battery life on either device to continue communicating with the world until you can get a new cord.

I've highlighted here the main strategies to implement to protect yourself and your business and make your time off as enjoyable as possible. If you want more information on working remotely, I highly recommend Timothy Ferriss' *The 4-Hour Workweek*. I will say upfront that as an editor, it's unlikely you'll ever be able to work a four-hour workweek, but you'll find many tips in Ferriss' book that could be valuable to you.

Because you are now self-employed as an editor, you have the advantage of flexible hours, time off when you need it, and the ability to work anywhere in the world you can find an internet connection. Life is short and we never know if we will have tomorrow. Take the time to enjoy this perk. Embrace the nomad editor lifestyle, and you'll create a lifetime of memories and invaluable experiences you would never have if you worked in an office for someone else.

Chapter 10
Working With the Stars

"Your best customers leave quite an impression.
Do the same, and they won't leave at all."

— SAP Advertising

DESPITE ALL THE work involved and usually going the extra mile for clients, and yes, occasionally becoming frustrated, for me, short of being able to support myself solely as a bestselling author, I can't think of any job that would better suit me than being a freelance editor. I would not trade it for any other job. I get to work from home or anywhere in the world I want. I have a flexible if busy schedule. I get paid well. I get to meet fascinating people. It may not be the made-in-heaven dream job, but it can be a darn good one. In this chapter, I'll share a few of my favorite experiences with some fascinating authors I've had the honor to work with.

I am often asked whether I've edited any books for famous people. I have never had the privilege of editing a book for a president or a major movie star, but I have had my brushes with some prominent and extremely interesting people. Here are a few of them.

James Donaldson is a former NBA All Star Player. He played for the Seattle Supersonics and San Diego (later Los Angeles) Clippers. He also played against greats like Kareem Abdul-Jabbar and Michael Jordan. At 7'2", you can understand why he decided to name his book *Standing Above the Crowd*. He was the first author who could claim celebrity status for whom I had the privilege of editing a book. Besides the fact that he is famous, his book makes clear that he cares a lot about his sport and also about his community, so I felt it was an honor to work with him.

Josh Wade was just starting out in his bodybuilding career when he hired me to edit his book back in 2009. He would go on to compete at the national level, including the Mr. Olympia contest more than once. Today he is a professional speaker, the owner of Team Wade Fitness, and a nutrition and fitness coach. And he's *huge*. Check out his book *Becoming a Stronger Person*.

Most know the name of movie star and martial arts legend **Bruce Lee**. Of course, Lee departed this world long before I became an editor. However, I was honored when Tommy Gong contacted me to edit his book about Bruce Lee, titled *Bruce Lee: The Evolution of a Martial Artist*. Equally as cool, Bruce Lee's widow, Linda Lee Cadwell, paid me to edit Gong's book. I have to admit I knew little about Bruce Lee at the time, but I learned a lot while working on this book, and today I can say I greatly admire Lee not only for his martial arts skills but also his philosophy about life.

Egan Inoue blew me away with his book *Being Relentless*. This guy has held the titles of World Racquetball Champion, World Mixed Martial Arts Champion, and World Brazilian Jiu-Jitsu Champion. Talk about diversity and athletic skill. Egan has even trained the stars of *Hawaii-Five-O* (the 2010 TV series). But what I really respect about Egan more than anything else is that he has refused to endorse alcoholic beverages, saying he does not want to set a bad example for youth and that alcohol has no place in professional sports. Egan sent me a shirt that says "Relentless, Egan Inoue." I wear it proudly because I feel I'm just as relentless in pursuing my writing and editing passion as he is in his athletic pursuits.

Rennie Davis is one of the great leaders of the 1960s Civil Rights and antiwar movements. As one of the Chicago Seven, he was put on trial for conspiracy to incite riot and other charges alleging he was a traitor to the United States following the protests at the 1968 Democratic National Convention. Davis not only helped to organize some of the biggest protests of the 1960s and 1970s, but he was close friends with John Lennon, met with world leaders, and traveled to Vietnam during the war. Today, he is writing a series of books to advocate for greater environmentalism and changes in our society, using methods that worked in the 1960s and 1970s. It was a true privilege to edit his first book *The New Humanity: A Movement to Change the World*.

Mary Flinn is one of the first authors I proofread a book for, and one of the rare ones who has since come back multiple times to have me edit her books—currently, nine and counting. Beginning with her novel *The One*, she has secured awards for nearly every one of her fabulous novels, which are much more than romance novels—they are introspective novels that get to the heart of relationships. I don't know anyone in her genre who writes better.

Laura Wharton was referred to me by Mary Flinn. Laura writes wonderful adult and children's mystery novels and has won a few awards herself. My favorite of her books—the first I edited for her—is *Leaving Lukens* about a small island off the coast of North Carolina and how it was affected by World War II. Her books are always fun, with an underlying, unexpected depth to them.

F. Celis Belina is a fascinating and downright nice man. He worked in Hollywood as an animal trainer and stunt man. He even worked on Tarzan films. I'm a huge Tarzan fan, so he sent me photos of former Tarzans he'd worked with. Check out his credits at IMDB. I thoroughly enjoyed editing his novel *Land of the Elephants* about a young woman in Africa who tries to protect elephants from being cruelly slaughtered.

Kim Ann Curtin decided it was time to reform Wall Street, and I was honored when she asked for my help. Her book *Transforming Wall Street* is partially a compilation of her own theories on how to change Wall Street following the 2007 recession. But she also interviewed dozens of people in the financial industry about how to reform Wall Street and promote what she calls conscious capitalism. Like so many other authors I've worked with, she is out to change the world for the better.

Randy and Michelle Rosado are a married couple who wrote a fascinating book titled *Pursuing Your Destiny*. It's a self-help book, but it's also the amazing story of how this couple met right after Michelle had survived being in the Twin Towers on 9/11. It was one of the first books published by a 9/11 survivor and is excellent reading.

Banana George (George Blair) made a name for himself at the end of his life by being the oldest barefoot water-skier on the planet. More than that, this man, who loved to wear yellow, also loved life and lived every minute of it, from racing cars with Prince Albert of Monaco to giving waterskiing performances for King Hussein of Jordan. Whether he was being interviewed by David Letterman or Oprah Winfrey or just handing out bananas in airports, he was an inspiration to millions. I never got to meet Banana George, but I had the privilege of working with his daughters on his biography, *Banana George: Don't Wait for Life to Happen, Make It Happen*.

Some of the most fascinating and enjoyable editing experiences I've had have been with authors who are from other countries and have migrated to the United States. Their stories of overcoming difficulties in their native lands and then adjusting to life in the United States are inspiring and make me feel like I have nothing to complain about. Here are just a few of these authors I've worked with:

In *Reflections of Gavea: My Epic Journey Home*, **Marianne Campagna** tells her one-of-a-kind international life story. Marianne was born to a German mother and Chinese father who met while her father was studying in Germany in the 1930s. They fled Germany to escape from Hitler's regime, eventually returning to China. Sadly, they then got divorced. In the divorce, Marianne's mother got custody of Marianne while her father got custody of her brother. Her mother then married a Russian count who had fled Russia during its revolution. When her mother and stepfather decided to immigrate to Brazil and flee the Communist Revolution in China, Marianne went with them. Growing up in Brazil and then moving to the United States, Marianne would lose contact with her Chinese family for decades. Her search and eventual finding of her father and brother is both heart-wrenching and heart-warming. I think it's one of the most incredible true stories ever told.

In *Evolving Through Adversity*, **Seconde Nimenya** tells the fascinating tale of her life growing up in Burundi, Africa. She lived through a civil war and came close to death a couple of times. Eventually, she married and moved to Canada and then the United States where she learned how to grow after a failed marriage. Then, she remarried her husband after she became a strong, independent woman.

The $2 American Dream by **Riadh Hamdi** is the true story of a Tunisian immigrant who was determined to make a better life for himself. He worked as a personal trainer in Tunisia, saved up his money to go on a tour of the United States, and decided he wasn't going back. The day the tour ended in Los Angeles and his fellow Tunisians returned home, he said goodbye to them and then went door to door in downtown Los Angeles with only two dollars to his name and knowing only one English word "job." Eventually, someone gave him a job and the rest is history. He worked his way up to manager, mastered English, and eventually became an entrepreneur. He is living proof that the American Dream does work.

I have edited several books by people with autism, bipolar disorder, depression, and anxiety. I have edited books for people with disabled children, people who care for elderly parents, and people who are cancer survivors. I have edited books for the blind and the deaf. I have edited books by LGBTQ authors—brave souls determined to change the world and achieve equal rights. I have edited books for people who have had a dream and pursued it until they have become millionaires, people who have spent their lives searching for God and claim to have found Him/Her, people who have dedicated their lives to helping the homeless, to being missionaries, to ending human trafficking, and countless other worthwhile endeavors. People who, in short, are extraordinary human beings.

All of these authors and so many others have inspired me to think differently and believe anything is possible through hard work and saying yes. I feel so many of them are kindred spirits because, like me, they refuse to quit but keep pursuing their dreams. I have loved working with all of them. In fact, even the most difficult authors have taught me something through their books and in my dealings with them, but that's a topic for the next chapter....

Chapter 11
Coping With Cannibal Clients

"Your most unhappy customers are your greatest source of learning."

— Bill Gates

ALL THAT GLITTERS is not gold. Sometimes what looks like it will be a plum project can turn into a nightmare. Sometimes you just can't predict how people will behave. I've had my share of experiences with cannibal clients—those who will eat up your time, eat up your money (by not paying you), or simply eat up your soul. Know the warning signs and avoid them. If you can't avoid them because you don't realize they have cannibal tendencies until you're enmeshed in the project, then do your best to cope with them. Following are some tips for how to do that.

Identifying Cannibals

Honestly, most authors you deal with do not act like cannibals. However, a significant number of them are uneducated about the publishing process and, therefore, will take up more of your time and potentially cause you a bit more frustration than they intend to. Therefore, I've broken this section into the three difficult types of clients you will likely have to deal with. The first two, inexperienced and high maintenance authors, are not truly cannibals, while the last type is out to get whatever they can from you, consciously or not, at the expense of your wellbeing. The inexperienced and high maintenance authors may frustrate you from time to time, but they will usually be appreciative of what you do for them and, overall, are well-meaning people who will just need some extra patience and guidance. If you try to turn them away, you'll likely lose a large percentage of your income, so I recommend you grin and bear it—and learn techniques to make working with them as painless as possible. In the end, their gratitude usually erases any discomfort you felt while working with them. The cannibals, however, you want to avoid as much as possible. Here are some characteristics of these different types of authors to help identify them and know what to expect when working with them.

Inexperienced Authors:

- Mail you files on flash drives or CDs, or heaven forbid, paper manuscripts, often with handwritten corrections on them.
- Don't know how to send an attachment in an email.
- When they do send attachments, will send you twenty-five emails, each with one attachment, each of which is a chapter of their book that you have to assemble because they don't know how to copy and paste their chapters together into one document.
- Don't know how to save the file you send them so when they open it and start making changes, they discover the next time they open it all their changes have disappeared.
- Don't know how to put in page breaks.
- May rite sensencesthat loo   liek this..

High Maintenance Authors:

- Don't know when to stop rewriting the book. They send you tons of corrections for the MS Word document—often in individual emails rather than in the document itself—and then tons more during the layout process.
- May seem like they are really easy to work with and will hardly make a change to the manuscript until it goes to layout or until the paper proof is received, and then they decide to rewrite the book. (Charge them extra in these cases.)
- Don't want to read your very clear and informative email. Instead, they will call you because they want you to explain the email to them as if they can't read English.
- Will call you to tell you they are sending you an email, or call you five minutes after they sent an email because you didn't respond yet.
- Will color-code their manuscripts. (You know, quotes are pink paragraphs, sections they are concerned about are green, discussion questions are blue, stories are orange, and then there are purple sections for reasons you can't discern but that they want formatted in special ways, which you know is a bad idea and will look unprofessional.)

- Rather than send you one file with all their testimonials in it, will forward each individual testimonial to you in the body of an email so you have to compile them all and fix all the formatting.
- Constantly want to set up appointments to talk to you or will call you more than once per day. They'll say it will be a quick five-minute phone call, but it'll be half an hour. Often, it is about something that could have been handled with a simple email.
- Will ask you the same questions over and over and not listen to you when you give them answers.
- Will continually ask you whether you think the book is good when you've already told them what you liked in it. In short, they are insecure.
- Want each chapter returned as you edit it. (Do not agree to do this. Edit the full manuscript and return it in one piece. You have enough to do without having to keep track of twenty-five attachments going back and forth, and if you find something in Chapter 17 that contradicts something in Chapter 3, it won't be easy to go back and update Chapter 3 if the author is currently reviewing it.)
- Will call you on weekends, during the evening, and even on holidays.

Cannibal Authors:

- May start out the relationship by demanding a discount—before you've even seen their book. (This is one reason to have a discount in your contract. People like to feel they are getting a deal.)
- Will want to negotiate your fees with you.
- Will want to make multiple payments over the course of many months but expect you to turn the work around in a month.
- Will not pay you on time and may not pay you at all.
- Will argue with you when you question a "fact" or statement in their books.
- Will demand you mail a paper copy of the manuscript to them.
- Will call you when they are drunk.
- Will call you at unreasonable hours such as before 8 a.m. or after 10 p.m., sometimes just to play psychological games with you.
- Will continually call and ask you questions before and after you send them an edit sample, wasting several hours of your time before they decide they can't afford your price or decide to hire someone else.

- Will claim they keep finding typos in your work because they don't know proper English and think your proper English is incorrect.
- Will claim your poor editing skills (see item above) constitute a reason not to pay you.

Coping with Cannibals

You can cope with all these types of authors, though some more easily than others. Inexperienced and high maintenance authors will likely reveal themselves to you when they first contact you. If your first contact is by phone, you may not realize their incompetence, but when you get the email full of typos and see the manuscript, you might have a good idea of what to expect. I never turn away these authors, but I do get a sense from my initial contact with them how much extra work it will be to help them, and then I add a bit to my price to cover it.

Fortunately, I have only worked with a few cannibal authors, but they have left quite an impression on me. In almost every case, I have just suffered through it until the book was done. I've usually still found their books interesting. If they are rude or obnoxious upon initial contact, such as drunk when they call me, I will quickly say no to them, but some of these people don't show their true colors until after the price is agreed on and the work begun.

Even if you have an agreement in place, if someone is making your life unreasonably difficult, you do not have to put up with it. Remember that you are working for you, so if someone is calling you names or swearing or yelling at you, terminate the relationship as quickly as possible. That said, some authors are just moody or cranky so you may be able to suffer through with them. (I usually try to feel compassion for them because they are so miserable, and that helps me bear the situation.)

Before you decide to end a relationship with a cannibal, take into consideration how this person came to you. I've occasionally had a cannibal author referred to me by a publishing coach or another client who has sent me many other clients. Because I want to continue my good relationship with the referrer, I put up with the cannibal client until the job is done. If this is impossible, explain to the person who referred the cannibal to you why you can no longer work with the client (never use the word cannibal except in your own thoughts); most likely, this person will understand. You also don't have to worry about the cannibal badmouthing you—cannibals who go around badmouthing people to their friends (if they are lucky enough to have any) will not be taken seriously since everyone will already know they are cannibals and will likely just feel sorry for you as the target of their misbehavior.

Occasionally, you do have to tell cannibals you can no longer work with them in the middle of the relationship. In that case, a short and simple email will do the job, such as:

> Dear X:
> We have very different personalities, and as a result, we seem to clash a lot. Therefore, I feel it is better that we no longer work together. I am returning the most recent version of your manuscript to you. I have already done more than two-thirds of the work agreed on and you have only paid me for half of the work, but I am willing to call it even. I wish you luck in finding someone else to help you complete it.
> Sincerely,
> Tyler

Keep the message short and to the point. If the cannibal complains, just repeat the same or similar message without engaging in an argument. Feel free to add, "Please quit contacting me," to your email if the cannibal is persistent. Do not give the cannibal any excuse to hook you into an argument or to try to sue you for not completing the work even though you have an agreement. If you are willing to lose a little money to end the relationship, cannibals will likely not complain since they know their behavior was atrocious and they are happy to have gotten something for nothing in terms of the extra work you basically did for free. I have never yet been threatened with a lawsuit for not completing a book, and I've only been in this situation a couple of times. On one occasion, the cannibal apologized to me for bad behavior, but never has a cannibal offered to finish paying me, so don't expect it. Eat your losses and be grateful you no longer have to work with the person.

Avoiding Cannibals

Obviously, you never know how authors are going to behave once you begin working with them. You can't even always avoid being cheated out of your hard-earned money. Trust me, I've been cheated out of money a few times. It was after experiencing such situations that I created my editing agreement. I should have had one right from the beginning, but I generally trust people and believe most people have good intentions and are honest. My agreement has largely solved my payment issues because I offer a 10 percent discount for paying in full. Most authors want to pay in full to get the discount, and then I don't have to worry about getting paid.

To the best of my knowledge, as an editor, you can't buy business insurance to protect yourself if someone tries to sue you. The best you can do is become an LLC, which, as I said earlier, I have never done. The likelihood you will be sued is minimal. I've never heard of a book editor being sued yet, and as long as your conduct is impeccable and you do nothing wrong beyond missing a typo, you should have nothing to worry about. If an author does threaten to sue you, simply offer a refund. Better to lose a few hundred or even a few thousand dollars and have it over with quickly than have a court case that will go on for months and that neither of you will win. I say neither will win because even if you do win, you will have lost time you could have spent doing work for other clients. Better to let your frustration and the money go. Forgive the cannibal in your heart and be grateful you no longer have to deal with the hostility.

As for the payment issues I have experienced, I now mostly refuse multiple payment plans, and in the few instances when I have agreed to them, I have made it clear I will not deliver the completed work until the final payment is made. It's either that, or if authors don't have the money to pay me half upfront, they will have to wait to have their books edited or find someone else. Some authors just want to purchase something they can't afford, and if they think they can afford a $700 monthly payment for five months, they are likely wrong. Plus, you'll probably have the book finished in two months, so why should you wait that long for your money? Remember, you are not running a charity; you're running a business, and you have as much right to eat as anyone else.

Furthermore, by having a signed agreement, the author knows you're professional and mean business; the agreement avoids any surprises down the road for both of you, and it will likely scare off the cannibals who realize you are not a wishy-washy person who will be an easy meal. I have yet to have an author refuse to sign my agreement, and with that agreement, I could always take an author to court for not paying me. As I said, I would never take anyone to court, but sometimes just making it clear it's a possibility will put people on their best behavior. Ultimately, real authors want to get their books published, so they'll do what is necessary to make that happen rather than try to pick a fight with you.

If you do end up working with a cannibal, when the book is finished, go back and analyze the relationship to determine what red flags existed before you started the work. Then you'll know better how to avoid a repeat of the situation.

Most importantly, when your experience with a cannibal is over, don't let it change the person you are. Focus on all the wonderful clients—even the inexperienced and high maintenance ones, especially if they happen to be really nice otherwise—who have been grateful for your help and sung your praises. Don't be a victim; become stronger for the experience. The world of editing is a wonderful place, and I have found that people in the publishing world are among the nicest there are. Nasty people exist in all fields, but overall, you have many blessings to count as an editor, so count them and move on.

Chapter 12
Plot, Characters, Action: Editing Fiction

"Edit your manuscript until your fingers bleed and you have memorized
every last word. Then, when you are certain you are on the verge of
insanity...edit one more time!"

— C. K. Webb

WHEN I FIRST envisioned becoming an editor, I pictured myself
editing novels. I love fiction and I write it myself. I never even
envisioned that I would spend most of my time editing nonfiction
books. I suspect less than 20 percent of my business is editing fiction, but I
still enjoy working on a good novel more than anything.

I have heard people advise authors not to hire an editor who edits everything, but rather, if you're writing a novel, you should go to an editor who
specializes in fiction. That may be good advice for an author, but it's lousy advice from an editor's point of view. If you want to eat, I suggest you accept the
books you are offered unless you feel extremely unqualified to edit them—as
I said, I don't edit cookbooks, children's books, or poetry, but I always take
memoirs, self-help books, business books, history books, etc. Would I rather
be editing a fantasy novel or a piece of historical fiction? Usually, but I have
edited some really fabulous nonfiction books too. Furthermore, in my case, I
am a novelist, so I'm usually writing or editing my own novels on a daily basis. I truly do think an editor who is also a published author will know more
about writing fiction than an editor who hasn't written a novel.

Once you become an established editor and have built up a clientele, if
you want to downsize or you want to narrow your focus to fiction or some
other genre only, that's great, but just know upfront that you likely won't be
able to start out only editing fiction.

Before you edit any fiction, I suggest you have a good grasp on the elements of fiction. If you're not a voracious reader of novels, then you probably shouldn't be editing fiction. Even if you are a big novel reader, you should understand the craft of writing fiction. I suggest you get some books on fiction and study them. Fiction basically falls into two categories—novels and short stories, and then there are many subcategories within those. For example, short stories contain flash fiction as a subgenre. Novels, of course, include the subcategories of science fiction, fantasy, historical fiction, mystery, romance, and many more, including subcategories within those subcategories. Become familiar with as many types of fiction as you can if you're going to edit it.

I'd also recommend you read some of the many fine books on writing fiction. Two of my favorites are the classics *Aspects of the Novel* by E. M. Forster and *The Art of Fiction* by Ayn Rand. A short and more current book is *Power Editing for Fiction Writers* by Carolyn V. Hamilton, which is basically a checklist of things authors can look for in their books to help them save money before the editor takes over. These books all discuss the basic elements of fiction like plot, characters, climax, and rising and falling action. Elmore Leonard's *10 Rules on Writing* can be read in less than ten minutes, but its advice is priceless. My favorite rule is "Try to leave out the part that readers tend to skip." And then there is Stephen King's *On Writing*. It also has excellent advice on writing fiction and writing in general. My favorite line in the book is "The adverb is not your friend"—a phrase I use time and again in explaining to clients why they don't need adverbs in their dialogue tags (something I'll talk about more below). There are also books about how to write in each of the subcategories I listed. Investigate some of them—you can easily find these books at Amazon and other booksellers.

I also highly recommend you try writing fiction yourself. Begin with writing a short story. Even though short stories are just that, they are extremely difficult to write because you have to condense everything. Many short story contests have a word limit, such as 2,500 words, so I recommend you try writing a story to that length. Then take that story and try expanding it to 5,000 words and try cutting it down to 1,000 to practice your plot and character development and also your ability to be concise. You'll find that this process is not easy, but it's great practice for both writing and editing skills. Honestly, I rarely write short stories because I tend to turn them into novels. And when I do write short stories, they are usually about characters from my novels. Some people are just born novelists, and I'm one of them. Writing novels is second nature to me. Perhaps you'll try your hand at short stories and discover you're a novelist too. Some might not agree with me, but I think the best editors are those who write regularly. I've often been complimented on how fast I edit—the reason I'm so fast is because I use my writing and editing muscles several hours every day. To be a good writer or editor, you need daily practice, just like you would to be a good athlete.

Not only do I recommend that you try writing some fiction, but I also recommend you join a writing group so you can get feedback on your writing. This will be invaluable for your growth as a writer and editor, especially because you will learn more about how readers react to fiction. That said, there is a real danger if you begin writing for the group and not for a larger audience. If you join a writing group, I suggest you only stay for a year and then join a different group so you get different opinions. Otherwise, you may risk caving in to someone like Joanie in your group. Joanie always complains about specific things, such as not liking stories told from the villain's point of view, or stories with magic in them, or stories with sex, or whatever. As a result, you learn to write stories that you know Joanie won't criticize; this situation does not help you or anyone else in the group. But you might also find a Beth in your group—someone whose advice is always spot on and invaluable. Leave the group, but cultivate the relationship with Beth outside the group—maybe the two of you can exchange pieces of writing on a regular basis and help each other.

When I edit, I don't just fix grammar and punctuation. I also try very hard to read like the target reader. I want the author to know how readers may respond to the work, so I write comments as I go along, letting the author know where I laughed, where I was grossed out, where I was cheering on the character, where I felt like crying, etc. I always provide reader-response comments with any book I'm editing, but it's especially important with fiction because readers become (or should if the book is well-written) emotionally involved with the characters, so the author needs to know how the story is affecting readers.

While I don't write mysteries, I once read an article that purported that every book is a mystery (even nonfiction books as I'll explain in the next chapter). In short, in a novel, from the opening sentence, readers should want to know how the main character will overcome the obstacle and achieve the desired goal. A good novel will keep that suspense running throughout the book so readers keep turning the page.

Here's a perfect example—the famous opening sentence of Jane Austen's *Pride and Prejudice*: "It is a truth universally acknowledged, that a single man in possession of a good fortune, must be in want of a wife." That sentence sets up the whole theme and mystery of the novel. We are soon after introduced to the Bennett family, and specifically the fact that there are five unwed and eligible daughters in the Bennett family and that a wealthy gentleman, Mr. Bingley, has just moved into the neighborhood. The mystery then is twofold: Which one of the Bennett sisters will end up marrying Mr. Bingley, and how that will come about? And then there are the plot twists—Mr. Bingley has a wealthy friend, Mr. Darcy. Which of the Bennett sisters will end up marrying him (another mystery)? And Mr. Darcy is rather obnoxious, so how will the selected Bennett sister overcome his obnoxious behavior and still fall in love with him? The clues (the development of the relationships) continue from there.

A good novelist keeps the reader constantly turning the page, wanting to know what happens next, wanting to find out how the mystery is going to be solved.

Modern fiction has little place for long-winded, Victorian-style chapters devoted solely to describing a house and the family. There must be very little telling and a lot of showing in a modern piece of fiction. Again, as Elmore Leonard says, "Try to leave out the part that readers tend to skip."

Obviously, as an editor you won't be writing a novel, just editing it, but chances are you may know more about writing fiction than the author. In fact, that would be the ideal situation if you are the editor. So share your expertise. A good editor doesn't just fix sentence structure or spelling errors but also lets the author know where the story works and where it doesn't and makes suggestions for how to fix the things that don't work.

Unfortunately, I have worked with several authors who have been given bad advice about writing fiction. They have been in writing workshops where their fellow participants, none of whom were published authors, took the scientific approach to writing that you must have x number of scenes of conflict in a story and they must happen at the x percentage points of the manuscript, etc. Frankly, I think this is largely balderdash. It's formulaic writing, and it does not work if you want to write a true novel. If you're writing genre literature—a thriller, a romance novel, a mystery—there is some degree of relevance to this kind of formula, but I always feel the authors who do not try to write a specific genre but rather a hybrid of genres are more successful. A novel cannot be written using a cookie-cutter concept unless you want it to be a dull imitation of someone else's novel. Years ago, I read the advice of Dr. Samuel Johnson, the great eighteenth century literary critic, on this matter and his advice is just as valuable today as it was 250 years ago:

There are three distinct kinds of judges upon all new authors or productions; the first are those who know no rules, but pronounce entirely from their natural taste and feelings; the second are those who know and judge by rules; and the third are those who know, but are above the rules. These last are those you should wish to satisfy. Next to them rate the natural judges; but ever despise those opinions that are formed by the rules.

Speaking of rules, when I came up with the title for this book, I realized *The Nomadic Editor* would be technically correct since nomadic is an adjective and nomad isn't. I was concerned some sticklers for good grammar might think, "What kind of editor has an ungrammatical title?" But I also knew *The Nomad Editor* had more of a ring to it and made my concept clearer. Since I know the rules and I very rarely break them, I thought I would take a liberty here. If Apple can do it with "Think Different," then I can too.

Plot and Character

Now that Dr. Johnson has spoken, we can discuss plot, since that is where the most rules are involved. Honestly, I don't care how many twists and turns there are in a plot. As of the writing of this book, I have published thirteen novels, and I have never once thought about how many scenes of rising action or conflict I would include in moving toward my climax. I do believe there needs to be rising action moving toward a climax, but I think the pacing of that is up to the author or the individual story. I don't honestly have a lot of advice to give on creating plot that will be helpful in editing, but in my opinion, a good editor will ensure a novel fulfills the following two criteria, and if it doesn't, the editor will make suggestions on how to accomplish this, usually through cutting, adding, and rewriting.

1. First and foremost, every chapter of a novel has to move the plot forward.

There's no time for dilly-dallying. Especially today, readers are extremely impatient and want to get on with the story. Now, especially if you are writing historical fiction, you may have an imposed structure to work from. In writing my novel *When Teddy Came to Town* about the Theodore Roosevelt libel trial that took place in 1913 in Marquette, Michigan, I plotted the novel over the course of the week that the trial took place. While my main character, Matthew Newman, had his own storyline, with his own angst and issues to work out, because he was a reporter attending the trial, he had to be present at all the trial scenes, and I had to follow the historical record of what happened at the trial and of Roosevelt's movements around Marquette when the trial was not going on. This gave me a natural frame for the book that controlled the rising and falling action. However, while the plot was taking place in 1913, much of the conflict was in my main character's head as he worked out issues based on his memories of living in Marquette three decades earlier. Events in the present triggered his memories of the past, and that allowed me to clue the reader in to situations that added to the tension, suspense, and rising action in the present, ultimately tying the trial and plot to my character's ability to come to peace with his past—a resolution he needed to achieve in the present. Every chapter and every scene in some manner developed the characters in ways that moved the plot forward.

2. Every chapter must in some way develop one or more of the characters.

It's extremely important to understand that by developing the plot, you are developing the characters, and by developing the characters, you are developing the plot. The two must be intrinsically tied together so that a character's personality determines the plot or the plot determines how a character will respond to a situation. For example, if my main character attends a dinner party, I show how the character speaks, acts, and reacts to other people at the dinner party. This may not help the character achieve his or her goal, but it does help us understand the character's strengths and shortcomings which will aid or stand in the way of achieving that goal. Since I often write regional historical fiction, I also try to make my scenes reflect interesting facts about the area or some sort of atmosphere about the region—these do not necessarily advance the plot or develop the character, but in my novels, I consider the region a character, so it needs to be developed as well, and the region plays a key role in my characters' motivations, depending on whether or not they grew up in that environment and how they react to it.

Ultimately, the character development should be the plot and vice-versa. Too often, I read beginning novelists' books where they are acting like writers and storytellers, telling us about characters, having fun developing a fictional world, telling us stories about the characters' lives, and basically writing episodic fiction that is almost a biography of the characters. However, this is not really writing a novel because it is largely plotless. Most beginning novelists also tend to write very biographical novels. They may be surprised if you tell them something in the story is boring or a scene doesn't develop the plot because everything in their book is based on real-life events, and they feel they should tell it like it happened even if they are pretending the book is fiction. It doesn't matter. Everything needs to move the plot forward and everything needs to develop the characters; the two are interdependent and cannot be separated. Too many books are character-based and then lack plot and too many are plot-driven to the point where the characters are one-dimensional caricatures or stereotypes. The true novelist knows how to integrate the two seamlessly.

As the editor, it is your job to look for places where development is needed. You can write comments telling the author that a scene goes nowhere so it needs to be cut, or you can suggest how it can be rewritten to advance the plot. You can point out that you don't understand a character's motivation for a certain behavior so the author can further develop the character to make the motivation clear.

Ultimately, it is not your book so you have to accept whatever decisions the author makes, and an author won't always take your suggestions, but you'll often plant a seed in a novelist's mind that will take the book into new and incredible places. Few things are more rewarding for an editor than to see this happen.

Head-Hopping

One mistake a lot of new novelists make—one I was guilty of myself until an editor pointed it out to me before I published my first novel—is head-hopping. This mistake occurs when novelists write in third person and show us the thoughts of all their characters. If you are writing in third person, only one character should be allowed to express thoughts in a chapter. If you need to show two characters' thoughts, create a separate chapter for the other character. Otherwise, you have head-hopping from one character's thoughts to another's. This situation is confusing for the reader, and worse, it can ruin the tension, since the reader knows what both characters are thinking while the characters don't. For example, if you have a scene where a couple are having a difficult discussion and you are writing in third person, it would be best to show it from one perspective. If you show the woman trying to convince the man that she is not yet ready to have sex, you can get deeply into her psyche—why she wants to wait, her fear of how the man will respond to her saying no, etc. The tension then lies in his reactions and her fears. Of course, the reader, to some degree, may know what he's thinking through the words he speaks, but rather than share his thoughts in that chapter, wait until you write the next chapter, after the conversation is over and the couple has parted for the evening, and then show us his reaction to the conversation by focusing the next scene on him. This makes both characters' individual viewpoints stronger and easier to follow. In such a scenario, I would also try to surprise the reader. You never want what will happen next to be obvious because it's boring. If the reader assumes the man is angry that the woman won't have sex in the chapter where we get her viewpoint, then in the next chapter, I might surprise the reader by revealing that the boyfriend was putting up a false front and is secretly relieved because he's actually gay, afraid to admit it, and nervous about trying to have sex with a woman. Such a surprise will only deepen the plot and characterization.

Point of View Shifts

I've edited lots of books written in first person where the author suddenly falls into describing something the main character cannot possibly know. The author has flipped from first person into third person in this case and has just ruined the willing suspension of disbelief by changing the point of view. Usually, an author makes this mistake to communicate some knowledge to the reader that is intended to be a surprise or not yet known by the main character. As the editor, it's best that you work with the author to figure out a way to reveal the information to the main character, or simply don't ruin the suspense by trying to build it up with something the main character is oblivious to. If a bomb is being planted, the surprise for readers is ruined if they are told the bomb has been planted. Let the main character, instead, experience the bomb going off, and then readers can react by sharing in the main character's shock and dismay. Or, if it's important to build suspense by letting readers know about the bomb, it might be best to switch to a third person narrative for the entire book. You can also drop in clues the main character sees that allow the reader and/or the character to be suspicious, but not really know.

Attention to Detail

A good editor will pay excruciating attention to detail, and in novels, that doesn't just mean punctuation or grammar, but also plot, character, and description.

I cannot tell you how many times I have discovered that I have contradicted myself when writing a novel. I write in a simple fact like the main character's favorite movie is *Gone with the Wind* and then a hundred pages later, I unwittingly state the character's favorite movie is *Yankee Doodle Dandy*, and not until draft four do I finally catch the inconsistency. Authors have a hard time catching these errors because they are so enmeshed in writing their books that they can't always remember what they said.

As an editor, you're more likely to catch these errors, and it is your job to do so. I once proofread a novel in which an engagement ring was stated to be

Victorian in an early scene. Then in the final scene of the novel, the ring was described as art nouveau. Neither the author nor the editor had caught this discrepancy, so the author was extremely grateful to me for catching it.

Historical facts—and really any facts—need to be checked for accuracy. In a novel I edited set in the 1880s, an elderly lady was living in an old house she had grown up in. The problem was that the town where she lived was founded in 1850, so if this old lady grew up in the house, she couldn't have been much older than forty. Worse, at one point, the character commented that she wasn't allowed to go to the movies when she was a child. I would hope not. Movies weren't invented until the 1890s.

Most authors won't make such glaring errors, but they may make some subtle ones. I once edited a novel set during the American Revolution in which one of the main characters was growing geraniums. Nope. Doesn't work. Geraniums weren't imported to the United States until after 1800. I've also edited novels set in medieval Europe where people are eating potatoes. Nope. The potato came from the New World so there weren't any in Europe before the sixteenth century. All of these little details need to be paid attention to. Question everything and look it up to ensure accuracy. Plants, vegetation, etc. change over time. Foods eaten today were not what people ate two hundred years ago. Clothing has changed. Technology has definitely changed. Few people owned a computer before the late 1980s. No one had a VCR in the 1950s. No one had a cellphone to take a photo with in the 1990s. These are all errors that authors writing in the twenty-first century might make because—believe it or not—they may not have been alive in those decades so they simply don't know what life was like then, or they simply never thought to double-check such facts.

Time is another detail that needs close attention. I've corrected errors in time zones where someone in Minnesota calls someone in Washington State and it's two hours later in Washington rather than vice-versa. I've read novels where someone in the United States calls someone in Pakistan when it would be the middle of the night in Pakistan, so the character isn't likely to answer the phone without at least sounding sleepy. Time zones also change during the year. For example, if you live in New York and call someone in Hawaii, it is six hours earlier there if it's Standard Time (spring to fall), but if it's Daylight Savings Time (fall to spring), it's only five hours earlier because Hawaii doesn't participate in Daylight Savings Time.

Time issues extend to dates and years. I'm a real stickler about using a calendar when writing and editing historical fiction. If an author writes that the date in the novel is February 14, 1913, I want to know what day of the week it is. It's easy enough to google "February 1913 calendar" and find out that Valentine's Day was on a Friday in 1913.

Of course, spelling is an extremely important detail. Question everything that seems suspicious. Look up the name of every type of handbag carried or every Pacific Island visited. Never trust an author to spell things correctly. Always assume it could be wrong until you double-check it. If there are alternate ways of spelling or writing something, pick one and make sure to use that spelling consistently throughout the book. Personally, I'm good with "Vietnam," but some writers insist upon "Viet Nam." That's fine so long as it's "Viet Nam" throughout the book and not "Viet Nam" on one page and "Vietnam" on another.

Dialogue

Nothing is worse in a novel than poorly written dialogue. Here are a few pointers to help authors fix their dialogue.

Use contractions: It's rare someone would say "I am going to the store to buy apples and I would like to know if you would like to come." More likely, the person would say, "I'm going to the store to buy apples, and I'd like to know if you'd like to come." That at least sounds human, although a more realistic sentence yet would be, "I'm going to the store to get apples. Wanna come?"

Avoid cheesy phrases no one really uses: I've edited books in which little boys say things to their friends like "Be a lamb and...." I have yet to hear a boy use that phrase in real life. If he did, his friend might just punch him. In another novel I edited, the author had her lovers continually calling each other "Darling." Does anyone really call anyone that anymore? The novel was set in the South and I'm from Michigan, so maybe they do in the South, but I've never heard anyone who wasn't in my grandparents' generation or older use that word when addressing someone. When I pointed this out to the author, she told me that people should call each other "Darling." I can't argue with that, but what should be and what is aren't the same thing, so best to stay realistic. At my recommendation, the author toned down the frequent use of the word.

A lot of these expressions like "Be a lamb" or "Darling" are used lazily because authors read them in Victorian novels or heard them in old movies. Such authors are writing based on how they think writers write rather than paying attention to how dialogue actually sounds. I love Jane Austen, but I admit the way her characters speak sounds stilted to me, despite how critics praise her ear for dialogue. Her contemporaries probably did speak like she writes in 1800, but people don't in the twenty-first century. Unless your novel is set in 1800, don't use Jane Austen as your dialogue model.

Adverbs and dialogue tags: Earlier, I mentioned that my favorite advice from Stephen King is, "The adverb is not your friend." This is especially true when it comes to dialogue tags. There is absolutely no reason to write a sentence like:

"Mary, run!" Joe shouted loudly.

That Joe is shouting is obvious from the words he says, the exclamation point, and the use of the word shouted. So leave out the adverb. After all, can you shout any other way than "loudly"? It's implied so not necessary.

Similarly, there's no need to write a sentence like:

"You know I love you," said Joe gently, while stroking Mary's hair.

Cut out the adverb "gently." The words Joe says and the fact that he is stroking Mary's hair make it obvious he is being gentle. Dialogue should always have within it the implication of how the speaker is speaking so the adverb is not necessary.

Similarly, authors should avoid overly descriptive words for the dialogue tags. There's no reason to say, "Joe ejaculated." If you want to say, "Joe shouted" or "Joe yelled," I can live with that, but we all know what image springs to mind when we see "ejaculated." Don't make your reader go there in the middle of your gunfight scene. Nor is there any need for "Mary prevaricated" or "Bob summarized" or "Ralph declared." Ninety-nine percent of the time, "said," "replied," and "asked," are the only dialogue tags you need. (Some writers will go so far as to say "said" is the only one needed.) Think twice before you use any others. When you use large words and adverbs in the dialogue tags, you distract the reader from the words the character is saying, and those words are the important part. Explain to your clients that the dialogue tag is not there to show off the big words they know. The dialogue tag is there to clarify who is speaking—it's utilitarian and that's all.

I've only hit a few of the highlights of writing dialogue here. Many fine books have been written on the topic and I encourage you to explore them. One I particularly recommend is *The Fiction Writer's Guide to Dialogue* by John Hough, Jr.

Word Choice

Never let an author use a big word when a small word will do. Notice I used the word "utilitarian" above. It's appropriate there. What isn't appropriate is using "utilize" when "use" does the job. "Use" can almost always replace "utilize," "utilization," or "usage."

One of the worst sentences I ever read described the main character as "standing on the border between land and fluidity." What this author meant was that the character was "standing on the beach." That's all that needed to be said. The whole book was written in such language, and I had a horrible time trying to follow what was happening.

Avoid jargon and company or industry speak and any big words intended to isolate your reader. Pick up an academic journal and you'll wonder whether the authors have any purpose in mind other than to intimidate their readers. If people outside of academia read that article, they would be either bored, frustrated, or pissed off. Read some business websites where companies describe the advantages of their products and you'll wonder what the heck the products actually do.

Too often the people who use such big words are simply trying to impress their readers with how smart they are, or they're full of bullshit and trying to cover up that they have nothing of value to say by using the biggest words possible to hide the fact.

Good communication is all about brevity. Teach the authors you work with to be concise and use the simplest words possible. Their readers will be grateful.

In Conclusion

There is so much more to writing good fiction, but I feel the tips above are the main ones you need to know. Do the best you can to suggest improvements for anything that needs improvement, and if you're working with a true beginner, suggest your author read some books on writing fiction or take a creative writing class depending on what is needed. Also, encourage authors to read some other books within their genres—and recommend only good books. I once had a pretty terrible author tell me he had become a better author in the last few years because he was reading as many as four novels a year. I had to laugh to myself because I tend to read at least that many in a month. In *James A. Michener's Writer's Handbook*, bestselling author Michener said, "I have long had the suspicion that no young person can become a writer who does not wear glasses by the age of twenty-three; failure to do so would mean that you hadn't done enough reading, and without ample reading I cannot see how one can ever become a writer." I don't think that's literally true—I didn't get glasses until thirty-one, but I must have had very healthy eyes because I spent many a night as a kid reading in the car as it grew dark and reading under the covers with a flashlight. Be honest with your clients and let them know they can't expect to have their first novel be a masterpiece unless they put in the work required by learning the elements of fiction and studying the best fiction possible. Yes, Margaret Mitchell's first novel was a big hit, but she spent ten years writing it, and she wrote many other stories and novels before it that weren't published until after her death.

In some cases, after doing an edit sample for an author, I have had to point out that there are so many problems with the novel that it would be pointless and a waste of the author's money for me to edit it. I would not be able to flesh out all the characters, scenes, and dialogue for the author because then it would be half mine. In some cases, the author has then wanted me to ghostwrite the novel, but I've always refused. In other cases, the author has thanked me for being honest and appreciated that I spent the time to write up a helpful summary of suggestions. Authors usually go back to the drawing board at that point. I may then receive an email six months or a year later telling me how much I helped and that the author has been reading and studying other novels and is still working on the book. I might not make any money from giving advice and turning away work in this way, but I feel better doing so than pretending the book is great and editing it, only to have it be published when I know it's terrible. I might make some money doing that, but the author will eventually get bad reviews and know I lied, and neither of us will feel good about it. Now and then you have to give some free help and write it off as a good deed. If you believe in karma like I do, you know the universe will repay you in other ways when you are honest and helpful.

Now let's turn to nonfiction, keeping in mind that many of the rules applying to fiction also apply to nonfiction, including the need for a plot.

Chapter 13
Organization and Transition: Editing Nonfiction

"There is no longer any such thing as fiction or nonfiction;
there's only narrative."

— E. L. Doctorow

I FIND THAT EDITING nonfiction often requires more intense labor than editing fiction. That's because fiction writers typically grew up wanting to write and have been writing for years. Consequently, they have a better sense of organization and their plots usually shape their novels' organization. That's not the case with nonfiction writers. Nonfiction lends itself to less organization, at least for certain genres like self-help and business books. Of course, a biography, autobiography, memoir, or history book will have built-in organization based on the chronology of the subject matter. Nonfiction writers are also not writing for the joy of writing but because they have information to share. They may not always know the best way to share that information through the written word, but they can still write books that are as powerful and life-changing as any novel—though they may need your help to do so.

As with fiction, if you're going to edit nonfiction, again, it doesn't hurt to read some books about writing nonfiction. Two of the best are *On Writing Well: The Classic Guide to Writing Nonfiction* by William Zinsser and Ayn Rand's *The Art of Nonfiction*. Below I will cover some of the issues I have had to help authors with in editing nonfiction, but I encourage you to explore further resources on your own.

Introductions and Conclusions

Most of the people I work with are first-time authors, so organization is rarely their strong point. They will often send me twenty chapters, several of which could be rearranged.

The thing is that even a nonfiction book has a type of plot. As mentioned earlier, I like to tell authors that all books are mysteries because the reader doesn't know where the book will go or what will be learned before reading it. Therefore, you have to plant clues for the reader as you go along. Those clues in a nonfiction book are more like signposts or mile markers so readers will know where they're going.

You probably remember the five-paragraph essay from elementary school and how it was structured: introduction, supporting evidence, supporting evidence, supporting evidence, and conclusion. A chapter in a nonfiction book follows much the same pattern except that part of your introduction and conclusion need to address where you've been and where you're going. For example, if you were writing a book about internet dating with women as your audience, Chapter 1 might be about the pros and cons of internet dating, Chapter 2 might be about selecting which internet dating sites are right for you, and Chapter 3 might be about how to set up your profile on a dating site. So when you get to Chapter 4: Beginning to Flirt, your introduction for that chapter might read something like:

> Now that you have your online profile in place and you have determined the personality you want to convey, you are ready to look for potential partners and also start responding to men who are interested in you. As you begin to get responses from people, you may decide to go back and adjust your profile to increase or decrease certain types of responses. In this chapter, we'll look at some scenarios of what might happen while flirting with potential partners on the internet and how to respond to men based on whether or not you want to continue the relationship. Then in the next chapter, we'll look at how to go from flirting online to in-person meetings.

This paragraph reminds the reader what happened in Chapter 3, and then gives a preview of what the reader will learn in Chapter 4 and even in Chapter 5. I repeatedly have to remind authors to write paragraphs like this because they have to understand that people are busy. Readers might have read Chapter 3 on Monday and not had a chance to read Chapter 4 until Friday, and by that point, they've forgotten where the book's discussion left off. In a book on internet dating, that might not be the case if readers are actively building an online dating profile while reading the book, but you'd be surprised how many people will read a book but never take action based on what they read, or they may simply read through the entire book first before they decide to take action. Therefore, we need to help readers remember what they read, whether the last time they picked up the book was before lunch or last month.

A chapter's conclusion paragraph needs to serve the same purpose. As I said, every book has a plot. In a nonfiction book, just like in a novel, you want to end a chapter with a cliffhanger that will make the reader want to read the next chapter. Let's use another example from our internet dating book. Let's assume that Chapter 5 of the book is called "Meeting in Person." Then when writing the conclusion to Chapter 4, you might write something like:

> By now you think Josh just might be the one for you. His profile shows you share the same interests. His picture makes him look attractive to you. He doesn't appear to have any red flags on his profile or in any of the messages you've exchanged. Now you've been smart and taken my advice to ask him for coffee, knowing you can easily escape if he turns out to be a psycho or just dull and boring, instead of meeting for dinner and being stuck with him for an hour and a half. Hopefully, he'll want to make a good impression on you, but how are you going to make a good impression on him? Don't worry; I've got you covered. In the next chapter, we'll explore how to dress appropriately for your casual coffee date, how to greet your date, and how to open a conversation without being awkward. I know you're ready to meet the man of your dreams in person, so let's get going.

Writing introductions and conclusions is not difficult, but you would be surprised how many authors never learned how to do so, or at least, just didn't pay attention to their sixth grade English teachers. Consequently, as an editor, I often will write in transition paragraphs, especially conclusions and introductions, or I will place a comment in the margin of the MS Word document to remind the author to write such a paragraph.

You might be surprised that I often write in paragraphs or even just sentences for authors. Well, it's a lot easier to write a paragraph that says what I think it should say than to write a comment trying to explain to an author how to write the paragraph and what it should say. I always let authors know it's their book, so they are free to reword anything I insert, and I always strive to write in the author's voice as much as possible, but ultimately, a lot of authors love that I write in sentences, transitions, and paragraphs for them. They are happy when I make them sound smart and make their sentences flow.

Organization

I swear a lot of authors write one draft and then send me their books without ever going back to see whether they make any sense. They also may have a poor concept of what the reader is likely to know or not know about the subject matter. They will go into great detail sometimes about something that is commonly known and doesn't require an explanation, and at other times, they will use an acronym that is specific to the industry they are writing about, but they never define what it stands for, so I don't know its meaning, and honestly, even the target audience may not.

These issues usually affect the book's organization. Authors often tell me to let them know if I have any questions as I work on the book, but I have found it is better to wait and ask the author questions once I've done one full edit. The reason is an author might drop a term or name in Chapter 1 that makes no sense to me, but in Chapter 6, it is explained. Instead, I keep a list of questions in a separate document, and then as I read, I usually find the answers to many of them. Then I can go back to Chapter 1 or wherever a term was first used and write in an explanation for it. For questions I don't find answers to, I insert comments in the margins asking the author to clarify them. Once I have the answers, I can go back and write in explanations where needed to make the text clear. Sometimes I will also have to rearrange things in the manuscript since it might not make sense to talk about a certain thing without something else being explained first. With most books, I don't do a lot of reorganizing, but at times, I move entire chapters, and then I have to renumber them and rewrite the transitions between them.

Even if I don't end up moving chapters, I usually suggest authors divide the book into parts so readers will have a better sense of the book's organization. When I say "suggest," I mean I will usually just divide it myself, inserting Part pages with titles for the parts. (If authors don't like it, they can always take them out.) For example, a book on internet dating might be divided into two parts—Part I: Online Setup and Communication, about creating your online profile and beginning to talk to prospective dates, and Part II: Going from Virtual to Real, which covers meeting your date in person and what to do from there. A biography might be divided into key periods in someone's life. For example, let's say I was writing a biography about a movie star who died fighting in World War II. The book might be divided as: Introduction, The Early Years: 1907-1925, College: 1925-1929, Depression: 1929-1933, Movie Star: 1933-1941, War: 1941-1944, and then be followed by a conclusion. Each of the sections, other than the introduction and conclusion, might have three, four, or more chapters. Depending on the book and how the transitions (conclusion/introduction) from one chapter to the next are handled, you might also want to suggest authors write short introductions or summaries for each section once you divide the book into sections. And while everything I change is a "suggestion," I still make the changes so authors can see what I mean rather than just trying to envision it for themselves. It's all undoable if authors aren't happy with the changes.

Bibliography Pages

Bibliography pages can be a thorn in an editor's side. Most authors have no concept of how to write a proper bibliography page. Some of them will try, but few will get it close to right. For self-help and business books that aren't really scholarly works, I've found simply adding a Recommended Reading list with just the title and author is sufficient. For example:

> *Creating Your Own Destiny* by Patrick Snow
>
> *Riches in Niches* by Susan Friedmann
>
> *The Nomad Editor* by Tyler R. Tichelaar

In a simple recommended reading list like this one, I would alphabetize by book title and list titles starting with A or The under A and T respectively.

For more scholarly works, I make sure the bibliography includes all the publication information—below is a book and an article example:

> Snow, Patrick. *Creating Your Own Destiny: How to Get Exactly What You Want Out of Life and Work*. Hoboken, NJ: John Wiley and Sons, 2010.
>
> Tichelaar, Tyler. "'Christabel': Coleridge's Conflict Between Christianity and Celtic Pantheism." *Michigan Academician*. 27 (1995): 493-501.

As I said, most authors won't know how to do this properly, so you need to know how. Make sure you study the specifics in whatever style book you're using for how to list items in a bibliography page.

You'll also find that authors have listed countless books you have never heard of or seen. That doesn't mean you have to run to the library to find them or ask authors to fill in missing information they usually won't know how to find. Instead, simply google most articles to find their bibliography information. As for books, my first resource is Amazon. If the book is listed at Amazon, it will usually have the search inside feature. Just click on the book cover and you'll see options to search inside; usually, the copyright page is one of those options. Be sure, however, that you select the paperback or hard-cover and not the Kindle version because the Kindle version often won't have copyright information. If there is no search inside feature for a book, scroll down the book's listing page at Amazon to the Product Details section; there you can usually find the name of the publisher and the date of publication. What you won't find there is the place of publication, but usually you can google the publisher to find its website and its contact information, including a mailing or physical address. Barnes & Noble's website also offers the same information; each book has a "product information" tab you can look on.

If you can't locate a book or article, leave comments in the manuscript for the author to find the information—hopefully, authors will have the books they used in their possession or have access to them. By using Amazon and Google as resources, I have not once gone to the library to find information for an author's bibliography page (and if I were to, I'd try my local library's online catalog first).

Indexing

Every so often, an author wants a book indexed. I have done both internal and external indexes for a few of my own books, but indexing is time-consuming, and if you use the internal index features in MS Word, it can be a hair-pulling out experience (and I have little hair left as it is), so I refuse to do it for authors. Instead, I refer them to an indexer. You may want to do some research or ask around to find a good indexer you can refer people to as needed. Create a relationship with the indexer; ask for a referral fee and offer to pay one for any authors referred to you.

Authors will also often ask whether it's important to have an index in their books. Truthfully, it depends on the book. If it's a history book, a biography of a famous person, a science book, or anything relatively academic, then yes, I would insert an index. If it's an autobiography or a self-help book, I would not. A business book is a maybe, depending on the subject matter and book's purpose. I do tell authors that if they are looking to sell their books to libraries, they should include an index. For example, if a library wants to buy a book on a specific topic and two books are available on that topic, the librarian will likely buy the one with the index. I know when I shop for history books or biographies, I want an index and will likely pass if the book doesn't have one.

In Conclusion

Editing nonfiction books can be a very rewarding experience. I have learned an awful lot about health and wellness, business strategies, dysfunctional behaviors, history, and many other topics from editing them. I have also helped many authors make books on those topics better. Remember, even nonfiction should have a narrative to keep readers interested in what might happen next. If you help authors create books that make readers want to keep turning the page, your clients will be happy because some of those readers will write positive reviews at Amazon, Barnes & Noble, Goodreads, and other online sites. And if authors are happy, they will likely refer others to you or come back to have you edit their future books.

Chapter 14
Helping Clients Sell Themselves: Writing Marketing Pieces

"The man who does more than he is paid for
will soon be paid for more than he does."

— Napoleon Hill

AS AN EDITOR, you may be asked to write and certainly will be asked to edit marketing pieces related to the book you're editing. Below are examples of marketing pieces I've helped authors create. Most are actually part of the book, but all these pieces help to market the book or market other services authors might offer connected to their books. Even if an author doesn't include these pieces, I always suggest them and help authors create them. Authors will be glad you are looking out for them and feel you are invested in their books.

Book Cover Descriptions

The first and most important marketing piece is the book cover's text. Most authors write a book but never even think about how to describe it on the cover. As a result, you can give the author pointers on how to write it, or you can write it yourself. I typically ask authors to write up a draft description of their books and then tell them I will tweak it. Sometimes, authors surprise me by writing such fabulous descriptions that I only change a few words, but more often than not, while I try to use the ideas they present, I tend to rewrite the entire description for them.

Here is what you will need to know and want to do in preparing the text for an author's book cover. We're assuming here the author will publish a hard cover with a dust jacket.

Front Cover

Obviously, the title and author's name go on the front cover. You will also want a subtitle if the book is non-fiction. The subtitle should further clarify what the title means. Here are some of my own nonfiction book titles with subtitles following the colons:

- My Marquette: Explore the Queen City of the North, Its History, People, and Places
- Haunted Marquette: Ghost Stories from the Queen City
- King Arthur's Children: A Study in Fiction and Tradition

If the book is a novel, it doesn't hurt just to add "a novel" below the title. Sadly, you would be surprised how many people do not clearly understand the difference between fiction and nonfiction. When I tell people I write novels, I am frequently asked whether they are fiction or nonfiction. Since I write historical fiction, some readers are confused and will ask me which house in Marquette (the town I usually place my novels in) my characters lived in. I then have to explain to them that my characters are fictional, and while I might have been inspired by a certain historical home when I described a house in a novel, that house is mostly a figment of my imagination. In any case, it never hurts to clarify on the front cover that it's a novel. Your intended audience will likely know "a novel" means the book is fiction. It's the non-readers who will usually ask you the clueless questions, but don't discount nonreaders—they often buy books to give as gifts to the readers in their lives.

You may also want a tagline on the cover. The tagline usually goes at the top above the title with the subtitle below the title. Examples of nonfiction taglines might be:

- Everything You Ever Wanted to Know About the Public School System
- Foolproof Tips for Creating the Life You Want
- Practical Advice for When Life Is Hard

Often the tagline and subtitle may sound similar or be almost interchangeable.

In place of a tagline, if the author has already written another book, you might want to include something like:

- By the author of The Marquette Trilogy
- By the award-winning author of *Willpower* and *Haunted Marquette*
- By the bestselling author of *I Did It!*

List books that prospective readers might already know and that will help identify the book as one by a favorite author.

Another option in place of a tagline is a short testimonial. When I say short, I mean short. One or two lines at most—nothing longer—so it doesn't detract from the cover image. For example:

"I fell in love with John Smith's characters and didn't want the book to end."

— Mary Harrison, author of *Love Comes 'Round Twice*

Or better yet:

"Page-turning excitement from cover to cover."

— *Book Nerd Magazine*

Back Cover

Ask your clients whether they want to publish hardcovers or paperbacks. This will determine what you put on the book's back cover. If the author is doing a hardcover, the book will likely have a dust jacket. Then I recommend putting as many testimonials on the back of the dust jacket as will conveniently fit without being too cluttered—usually three to six, depending on length. Put a line at the top that says something like:

- Praise for *The Only One*
- What Readers Are Saying About *A Good Book Is Hard to Find*
- Why Readers Are Raving About *My Secret Vampire Boyfriend*
- What People Are Saying About John Smith and *Exploring Your Options*
- Fellow Hypnotists Praise *You're Getting Very Sleepy*
- Why Other Doctors Recommend *You Are What You Eat*

Beneath whatever heading you choose, list all the testimonials. Again, you want to keep these short. They can run to three or four lines, including the author tag, but not more. If you keep them shorter, you can fit more on the back. A typical back cover may hold up to 300 words, but when the book goes to the book designer, the layout might change how many will fit, so let authors choose which ones they want on the back cover, and let them know to put them in order so the ones they can live without are at the bottom. Those testimonials might be cut if the cover designer has an image on the back or there just simply isn't enough room for them. Even if the testimonials are placed on top of the image, they might be hard to read, so be prepared to select only the very best testimonials.

Typical testimonials might look like this:

"I've worked with Hannah Buell for seventeen years, so I know every word in this book comes directly from her heart. I've watched how much she cares about her clients and the incredible results they get, so I can, without reservation, recommend *Get in Shape Now* as a life-changer."

— Delores Quincy, Personal Trainer, Hot Bodies Gym, Los Angeles

Make sure the author tagline is not longer than the quote. What you don't want is:

"This book is a must-read!"

— Kevin Fagin, Owner of Fagin Consulting, President of the Toledo Commerce Club, and Author of *Maximizing Your Retirement Nest Egg: A Guide to Investing for Baby Boomers to Millennials*

You'll find that most of the people who write testimonials for your client will not know much about writing them and will often want to promote themselves, so let the author know when requesting testimonials to tell people their testimonials are subject to editing and can only include one credential. The author will likely end up with three to thirty testimonials. Tell authors to aim for ten. No one wants to read thirty. Ten is enough to convince readers it's a book worth reading. Also, when you edit the testimonials, watch for phrases like "must-read" which several people will likely use to describe the book. It's a worn-out saying, but okay to include provided no more than one person giving a testimonial says it.

If the author is doing a hardcover, then the testimonials are enough for the back cover. However, if the author is doing a paperback, put the testimonials in the front pages of the book before the title page (just like in this book). You may opt then to put one testimonial on the front or back cover so at least one is visible without opening the book. Since you want ten testimonials ideally, if the author is doing a hardcover with a dust jacket, tell the author to pick the best four testimonials for the back of the dust jacket and then the rest can go inside the front cover before the title page.

There absolutely needs to be a description of the book somewhere. I can't tell you how many self-published books I've seen that have blank back covers or back covers with testimonials, but no description of what the book is about or what benefit the reader will get from it. If I don't know what a book is about, I won't buy it. Not having a description of the book is, in my opinion, the biggest mistake an author can make when printing a book, so don't let the authors you work with get away with not putting a description on the cover if there are no flaps.

Inside Front and Back Flaps

If the author is doing a paperback, there will be no flaps or dust jacket unless the author decides to do French flaps (flaps that are part of the actual paper cover and fold inward to make the paperback a hybrid of a hardcover and paperback. And let me just say here that I hate reading a book with French flaps. Yes, they will cost less than a dust jacket, so some authors opt for them, but they have a tendency to flip open so that the book is awkward to hold and read.) If the book is a paperback, the text normally put on the flaps should go on the back cover, which is why the testimonials are moved to the inside front pages.

If there are flaps, there will be a front and a back flap. Here's what you want to do with each:

Front Flap: It should contain the book description. Typically, about 250 words will fit on the front, inside flap. I have seen some horribly written book descriptions, so it's important to get this right. Do not just quote a passage from the book that fills the entire flap. A very short excerpt is okay, but never let an excerpt replace a description.

Remember that the flap is a marketing piece so you want relatively short paragraphs that grab readers' attention right away and make them feel they have to read the book.

Below are suggestions for writing both nonfiction and fiction descriptions for back covers, along with some examples.

Nonfiction Descriptions

If the book is nonfiction, the text should address the problem readers may have and convince them that, by reading this book, they will be able to solve it. I typically write two short paragraphs about the book, beginning with a question or two, such as "Are you tired of feeling overwhelmed all the time?" to engage readers, and then I include a sentence like "In *Get Your Life Back*, you will learn how to:" followed by a series of bullet points such as:

- Say "No" to things you really don't want to do
- Eliminate toxic people from your life once and for all
- Find the courage to follow your passion

Typically, I'll write about 6-8 of these bullets, depending on the space allotted and how long the paragraphs might be. It's important to use verbs to start each line or "how" and "why" phrases. Often, you can just reword the chapter titles a bit to create the bullets, especially if it's a business or self-help book.

If it's a history book or something more academic in nature, I wouldn't use the bullet points but just a few short, tight paragraphs that clarify what the book is about.

Following are a few examples of full back cover texts I've written for my own books:

Description for The Gothic Wanderer

The Gothic Wanderer Rises Eternal in Popular Literature

From the horrors of sixteenth century Italian castles to twenty-first century plagues, from the French Revolution to the liberation of Libya, Tyler R. Tichelaar takes readers on far more than a journey through literary history. *The Gothic Wanderer* is an exploration of man's deepest fears, his efforts to rise above them for the last two centuries, and how he may be on the brink finally of succeeding.

Tichelaar examines the figure of the Gothic wanderer in such well-known Gothic novels as *The Mysteries of Udolpho*, *Frankenstein*, and *Dracula*, as well as lesser known works like Fanny Burney's *The Wanderer*, Mary Shelley's *The Last Man*, and Edward Bulwer-Lytton's *Zanoni*. He also finds surprising Gothic elements in classics like Dickens' *A Tale of Two Cities* and Edgar Rice Burroughs' *Tarzan of the Apes*. From Matthew Lewis' *The Monk* to Stephenie Meyer's *Twilight*, Tichelaar explores a literary tradition whose characters reflect our greatest fears and deepest hopes. Readers will find here the revelation that not only are we all Gothic wanderers—but we are so only by our own choosing.

"*The Gothic Wanderer* shows us the importance of its title figure in helping us to see our own imperfections and our own sometimes contradictory yearnings to be both unique and yet a part of a society. The reader is in for an insightful treat."

— Diana DeLuca, Ph.D. and author of *Extraordinary Things*

"Make no mistake about it, *The Gothic Wanderer* is an important, well researched and comprehensive treatise on some of the world's finest literature."

— Michael Willey, author of *Ojisan Zanoni*

Description for Haunted Marquette

Paranormal/History $19.95 U.S./Canada

"*Haunted Marquette* deftly weaves history, urban legends, and unexplained phenomena into a kaleidoscope of ghostly hauntings that reveal a side of the Queen City most of us have never experienced but perhaps always feared was there."

— Sonny Longtine, author of *Murder in Michigan's Upper Peninsula*

Over Forty Tales of Ghosts and Paranormal Experiences

Founded as a harbor town to ship iron ore from the nearby mines, Marquette became known as the Queen City of the North for its thriving industries, beautiful buildings, and being the largest city in Upper Michigan. But is Marquette also the Queen of Lake Superior's Haunted Cities?

Seventh-generation Marquette resident Tyler Tichelaar has spent years collecting tales of the many ghosts who haunt the cemeteries, churches, businesses, hotels, and homes of Marquette. Now, separating fact from fiction, he delves into the historical record to determine which stories may be true and which are just the fancies of frightened minds.

Read the chilling tales of:

- The wicked nun who killed an orphan boy
- The librarian mourning her sailor lover
- The drowned sailors who climb out of Lake Superior at night
- The glowing lantern of the decapitated train conductor
- The mailman who gave his life for the U.S. mail
- More ghostly ladies in floor-length white gowns than any haunted city should have

Haunted Marquette opens up a fourth dimension view of the Queen City's past and reveals that much of it is still present.

Fiction Descriptions

While I would not quote an excerpt from a nonfiction book in the cover's description, a novel is different. If you can find a short, effective passage, go ahead and use it.

Here are examples of cover descriptions for two of my novels, both of which begin with a quote from the novel, which I put in italics.

Description for Iron Pioneers: The Marquette Trilogy, Book One

Back in Boston, the thought of settling in a new land had seemed a romantic adventure to share with her new husband. Now, despite the lush green trees, and the sandy golden beaches, she began to fear what wild animals or unfriendly Indians might lurk in those woods, and she sensed the loneliness to come of being so far from her family.

When iron ore is discovered in Michigan's Upper Peninsula in the 1840s, entrepreneur Gerald Henning and his beautiful socialite wife Clara travel from Boston to the little village of Marquette on the shores of Lake Superior. They and their companions, Irish and German immigrants, French Canadians, and fellow New Englanders dream of a great metropolis at the center of the iron ore industry. Despite blizzards and near starvation, devastating fires and financial hardships, these iron pioneers persevere until their wilderness village first becomes integral to the Union cause in the Civil War and then a prosperous modern city.

Meticulously researched, warmly written, and spanning half a century, *Iron Pioneers* is a testament to the spirit that forged America.

Description for Arthur's Legacy: The Children of Arthur, Book One

He felt suddenly as if a siren's song were calling to him from across the sea, from an enchanted land, an island kingdom named England. He had always pictured England as a magical fairy tale realm, ever since his childhood when he had first read the legends of King Arthur and the Knights of the Round Table.

Magic existed in the thought of England's green hills, in the names of Windsor Castle, Stonehenge, and the Tower of London. It was one of the few lands still ruled by a monarch, perhaps a land where fairy tales might still come true. Maybe even a place where he might at last find a father.

All his life, Adam Morgan has sought his true identity and the father he never knew. When multiple coincidences lead him to England, he will not only find his father, but mutual love with a woman he can never have, and a family legacy he never imagined possible. Among England's green hills and crumbling castles, Adam's intuition awakens, and when a mysterious stranger appears with a tale of Britain's past, Adam discovers forces may be at work to bring about the return of a king.

There is key information you want to clue the reader in to when writing the back cover description for a novel. For example:

- Who is the main character?

- What is the setting?
- What is the situation the main character is in?
- What is the main character's goal or motivation?
- What obstacles will the main character overcome in the novel?

Be careful not to give away too much. You can hint at what the character will learn or what the dangers might be, but don't say much that goes beyond what happens in the first third of the novel.

Back Flap: Here I would place an author photo, which will take up about half the space. Then put a short About the Author paragraph or two below that. I usually ask authors to write a three- or four-paragraph biography of themselves in third person to put in the back of the book as the About the Author page. I then trim that down to about 100 words to fit on the back flap, leaving the longer biography in the back of the book. You can only fit about 100 words on the back flap if you want to leave room for the author photo and not make the flap look too cluttered.

Genre, Price, and Website: I would leave the placement of these up to the author and layout person, but typically, the genre and price are on the inside flap above the description, or they may be near the barcode. It is imperative to list a genre. You can go to www.bisg.org, the website for the Book Industry Study Group, to see its complete listing of BISAC (Book Industry Standards and Communications) codes, the main genre codes used in the book industry. However, you do not necessarily have to use one of these codes. No one is paying attention to how you list the book's genre. The important thing is to be accurate about it so bookstores, both brick-and-mortar and online, know where to list the book. For nonfiction books, I usually list two genres, such as: Business/Computer Systems, Careers/Personal Development, Self-Help/Relationships, History/Medieval.

For novels, standard genres are Fiction, Literary Fiction, Historical Fiction, Romance, Science Fiction, Fantasy, and Mystery. You may want to be more specific such as Paranormal Fiction, Historical Fantasy, Thriller, Suspense, etc. Ask authors to look at the genre listings for books similar to theirs to determine what the best genre choices would be.

Place the website address at the bottom of one or both flaps or on the back cover at the bottom if there are no flaps. Include the website address so readers can find out more about the book if they don't buy it when they first see it; plus, a website address is an invitation to learn more about authors and explore their other books.

Other Items: Other items you might include on the cover are credits for the editor, cover designer, and layout person, and for the cover or author photos. These are optional on the cover, and if you include them, I'd put them on the back flap below the author bio. If you don't include them on the cover, be sure to include them on the acknowledgments page and/or copyright page.

Sales Pages for the Back of the Book

Following the About the Author page, I often encourage authors, especially those writing nonfiction books, to add in advertising pages for their services. The following are a few examples. The first example I recommend placing in all books because book reviews are not easy to get so a nudge to the reader never hurts. Next are descriptions of the author's other books—these are usually shortened versions of back cover text. The rest depend on the kinds of services authors provide.

Thank You for Reading
Haunted Marquette!

If you enjoyed this book, please consider writing a short book review at Amazon, Barnes & Noble, or another online bookseller's website. Book reviews are the best way, along with word-of-mouth, to help a book's sales and show your appreciation for the author's hard work. Even just a few words or a sentence or two can make a difference in helping an author.

Also, if you have had your own ghostly encounter in the Marquette area, I would love to hear about it. Email me at tyler@marquettefiction.com to tell me your story and possibly have it included in a future edition of this book or a sequel.

May all your hauntings be fun and meaningful!

Tyler R. Tichelaar

Be Sure to Read All of Tyler R. Tichelaar's Books
IRON PIONEERS:
THE MARQUETTE TRILOGY: BOOK ONE

When iron ore is discovered in Michigan's Upper Peninsula in the 1840s, newlyweds Gerald Henning and his beautiful socialite wife Clara travel from Boston to the little village of Marquette on the shores of Lake Superior. They and their companions, Irish and German immigrants, French Canadians, and fellow New Englanders face blizzards and near starvation, devastating fires, and financial hardships. Yet these iron pioneers persevere until their wilderness village becomes integral to the Union cause in the Civil War and then a prosperous modern city. Meticulously researched, warmly written, and spanning half a century, *Iron Pioneers* is a testament to the spirit that forged America.

THE QUEEN CITY
THE MARQUETTE TRILOGY: BOOK TWO

During the first half of the twentieth century, Marquette grows into the Queen City of the North. Here is the tale of a small town undergoing change as its horses are replaced by streetcars and automobiles, and its pioneers are replaced by new generations who prosper despite two World Wars and the Great Depression. Margaret Dalrymple finds her Scottish prince, though he is neither Scottish nor a prince. Molly Bergmann becomes an inspiration to her grandchildren. Jacob Whitman's children engage in a family feud. The Queen City's residents marry, divorce, have children, die, break their hearts, go to war, gossip, blackmail, raise families, move away, and then return to Marquette. And always, always they are in love with the haunting land that is their home.

SUPERIOR HERITAGE
THE MARQUETTE TRILOGY: BOOK THREE

The Marquette Trilogy comes to a satisfying conclusion as it brings together characters and plots from the earlier novels and culminates with Marquette's sesquicentennial celebrations in 1999. What happened to Madeleine Henning is finally revealed as secrets from the past shed light upon the present. Marquette's residents struggle with a difficult local economy, yet remain optimistic for the future. The novel's main character, John Vandelaare, is descended from all the early Marquette families in *Iron Pioneers* and *The Queen City*. While he cherishes his family's past, he questions whether he should remain in his hometown. Then an event happens that will change his life forever.

All books are available at www.MarquetteFiction.com

Life Coaching

Create the life of your dreams with the guidance and accountability of an experienced success coach! Brandon Wiseman, MBA, is a success coach specializing in the areas of academics, careers, business, and leadership. After owning and operating his own multi-million dollar real estate company for twenty-five years, Brandon is now ready to share with you how you can also pursue your dreams and achieve your goals.

Through his life coaching practice, Brandon will help you or your loved ones get ahead in life while maintaining your life balance. Whether you're looking for guidance in your studies, you are ready to launch your career or small business, or you just want to take your leadership skills to the next level, Brandon can show you the ropes and help you revolutionize your lifestyle.

Group Coaching and One-On-One Coaching plans are available. Packages come in one-month, six-month, one-year, multi-year, and lifetime combinations. Visit brandonshouse.com or email Brandon at brandon@brandonshouse.com for more information.

Wish Fulfillment Consulting

With graduate degrees in Business Administration and Social Work, Marie Davenport works with schools and colleges to unlock students' potentials and guide them to success. Having started her career in teaching, Marie has the unique skills needed to guide institutions at a high level through transitory times.

Available for consulting work, conducting institutional studies, developing strategic or tactical plans, and conducting faculty or staff development workshops or seminars, Marie will help you bring out the best in your students and staff so they can reach their highest potentials.

Whether you are undergoing a campus reorganization, implementing a new curriculum, or just looking for someone to inspire your staff, Marie will draw upon her business, education, and social work skills to create a success plan for your business or institution.

To find out how Marie can help you or your organization, contact her at:
marie@wishfulfillment.com
616-xxx-xxxx

Book Joanne to Speak at Your Next Event

As a gifted and prolific speaker and entertainer, Joanne Demilio draws on her years as a single mother, career woman, and new grandmother to craft a unique presentation for your audience.

With thirty-five years of expertise in leadership, corporate America, and the family kitchen, Joanne knows how to balance work and personal lives, productivity and health, and still leave time to meditate or go for a jog.

Joanne's humorous message of survival amid chaos in the home will leave your audience members laughing and wanting more. But most importantly, they will learn new skills and strategies for balancing their lives, eliminating frustrations, and embracing anew their life missions with gratitude.

Contact Joanne today for a complimentary thirty-minute consultation to learn how she can help make your event an overwhelming success.

1-888-xxx-xxxx

joanne@funnybusinesslady.com

Note that these last few kinds of pages are especially effective for non-fiction books because the authors are probably less concerned about selling books than using them to show they are authorities in their fields so people will hire them to speak or do consulting work—where the big bucks are. If you're editing nonfiction books, I highly recommend you suggest authors include such pages and you help them write them.

Other Marketing Pieces

As I said, the text for the front and back cover and any flaps is the most important marketing piece you will create for the author. I always include it, plus sales pages, in my initial price quotes.

Authors, however, may ask you to help them create other marketing pieces such as sell sheets, speaker sheets, or press releases. They will usually ask for this after their books have gone to the printer. Do not agree to do these for free—if you do, then they will keep asking you for more and more. Instead, set a standard price for editing or helping to write these items. In some cases, authors might create the text themselves and then just want you to edit it, in which case, just charge your hourly fee for however long it takes to do the work.

If you are going to write these yourself, I suggest you set a reasonable price for the work, such as $100, assuming it won't take you more than a couple of hours to write up the text and work with authors on changes they might want to make. Most of these items will be 500 words or less, so they don't take long to write, but they do take a while to tweak and make perfect. By this point, you will also know whether the author is easy to work with or is likely to want to reword the text six times, so you can charge accordingly when you give a quote. Be willing to count the first few attempts as a learning experience. It might take you longer to write the first few than it will once you have a dozen or so under your belt. You can then adjust your pricing down the road to what you feel is fair.

Press Releases: Authors often ask me to write press releases for them. Plenty of information is available on how to write a good press release and you might already have experience doing so. I'll simply include a few examples of press releases I've written for my own books and remind you that press releases should be about one page.

For Immediate Release

Local Author Tyler Tichelaar Releases New Book about
Haunted Marquette

October 2, 2017—Local author Tyler Tichelaar will be giving his readers a treat this Halloween season. On Wednesday, October 11 at 6:00 p.m. at the Marquette Regional History Center he will be releasing his newest book, *Haunted Marquette: Ghost Stories from the Queen City.* The book contains more than forty stories of ghosts and paranormal activity within the city of Marquette.

"For years I've heard stories of various hauntings and collected them," says Tichelaar. "I never thought I'd have enough for a book, but as I interviewed people, one story led to another. I've found sufficient evidence to make me believe several buildings in Marquette may be haunted or have experienced hauntings in the past."

Haunted Marquette is divided into several sections on hauntings in Marquette's churches and cemeteries, the downtown businesses, the lakeshore, various houses, and Northern Michigan University. Tichelaar researched each location to determine the likelihood of a haunting there and whether any historical evidence existed to make the haunting plausible. He also interviewed numerous people about their personal experiences with ghosts.

"I was afraid I would end up talking to a bunch of crazy people when I set out to write this book," said Tichelaar, "but everyone I talked to was very sincere. Not one of them was seeking attention; most had not believed in ghosts before until they had a strange experience they could not explain logically."

Numerous city landmarks are highlighted in the book as locations where ghosts have been sighted, including the former Holy Family Orphanage, Park Cemetery, the Marquette lighthouse, the Landmark Inn, the Peter White Public Library, and the Thomas Fine Arts building at NMU.

"Only a couple of the hauntings can really be described as frightening," says Tichelaar. "Most of these stories are about unexplainable phenomena; a few are heart-wrenching when you realize the tragedies some of the alleged ghosts experienced while still human, which has caused them to linger on this earth."

Tichelaar will release *Haunted Marquette* at the Marquette Regional History Center on Wednesday, October 11. A presentation will begin at 6:00 p.m. and last about an hour, followed by a book signing. Partial proceeds from the book signing will be donated to the history center.

Tyler R. Tichelaar is a seventh generation Marquette resident. He is the author of The Marquette Trilogy, *My Marquette*, and numerous other books. In 2011, he received the Outstanding Writer Award in the Marquette County Arts Awards, and the Barb H. Kelly Historic Preservation Award. His novel *Narrow Lives* won the 2008 Reader Views Historical Fiction Award. In 2014, his play *Willpower* was produced by the Marquette Regional History Center at Kaufman Auditorium. You can learn more at Tichelaar's website www.MarquetteFiction.com and at the Marquette Regional History Center's website www.marquettehistory.org.

###

New Historical Novel Explores Orphan's Seven-Decade Journey

Amid a cast of unforgettable characters, and from the Great Depression to Finn Fest 2005, Lyla Hopewell survives a childhood in an orphanage and seeks her identity and the love she's always craved in Tyler R. Tichelaar's new novel The Best Place.

Marquette, MI July 6, 2013—An irritating best friend gained during a childhood spent in a Catholic orphanage, a father who became a Communist and migrated to Russia in the 1930s, and 3:00 a.m. visits to The Pancake House. Such is the life of Lyla Hopewell. But things are about to change for her in Tyler R. Tichelaar's new novel *The Best Place* (ISBN 9780979179075, Marquette Fiction, 2013).

During the Great Depression, many American Finns migrated to Karelia, a Finnish province under Soviet control. Convinced the American Dream was a falsehood, they were ready to embrace Communism, and Lyla Hopewell's father was among them. Planning to send for his wife and daughters once he was settled, he was never heard from again. Then Lyla's mother died, her sister was adopted, and she was sent to a Catholic orphanage.

These inauspicious beginnings gave Lyla plenty of reason to be ornery, but they also made her tough. Now at age seventy-seven, Lyla will find her past intruding into her present. She'll try to reconcile with her ex-boyfriend, be badgered by her best friend into joining a women's recovery group, be harassed by a foul-mouthed teenager, and embrace her heritage at Finn Fest 2005.

Tyler R. Tichelaar's novels have won fans across North America. Canadian author Laura Fabiani describes his books as "Never predictable, sometimes heartbreaking, always hopeful." Laura Johnson of Review the Book (Austin, TX) states, "I have found a new favorite writer.... The writing is fresh, yet it has a feel of the old, historical novels of ages past." And Bethany Andrews of Book of the Moment (Maine) declares, "I am now and forever a huge Tyler Tichelaar fan. He's a man with a wonderful gift for storytelling, and a knack for presenting historical facts in a way that can rival any great historical fiction author."

In *The Best Place*, Tichelaar has created a tour-de-force with memorable characters, many returning from his previous novels, who reflect the insecurities, fears, hopes, and dreams we all have. *The Best Place* is Tichelaar's funniest, most heart-wrenching, and overall most cathartic novel to date. Lyla Hopewell's story of survival and resilience amid personal mistakes, rejection, and life's obstacles will inspire readers from all walks of life.

About the Author

Tyler R. Tichelaar, PhD in Literature and current president of the Upper Peninsula Publishers and Authors Association, is a seventh generation resident of Marquette, Michigan, the city where his novels are set. In 2009, Tichelaar received the Best Historical Fiction Award in the Reader Views Literary Awards for his novel *Narrow Lives*. In 2011, he received the Barb H. Kelly Historic Preservation Award from the Marquette Beautification and Restoration Committee for his book *My Marquette*, and he received the Marquette County Arts Award that same year for "Outstanding Writer."

The Best Place (ISBN 9780979179075, Marquette Fiction, 2013) can be purchased through local and online bookstores. For more information, visit www.MarquetteFiction.com. Review copies available upon request.

Note: I do not distribute press releases for clients, but they often ask me to. I refer them to Reader Views or any of the other online PR sites available. I also encourage them to distribute their press releases to all their local newspapers and TV and radio stations.

Sell Sheets: Sell sheets are great for authors who want to get into public speaking and want a professional-looking marketing piece to send to event planners or the media. Typically, a sell-sheet should be two-sided, front and back, and full color. I am not a graphic design artist, but I know with sell sheets, the graphics are as important as the words. I typically write up a sell sheet with instructions for where to include graphics, such as the author pho-to, a book image, possibly a company logo if the author has such, or some fun images. For example, if the author is a basketball coach, you might suggest including a basketball or basketball hoop image. If the author is an inventor, maybe include an image of an invention or a light bulb to symbolize bright ideas. Be flexible about this—the graphic designer will likely come up with something different and better than what you initially envision, but it's good to provide some ideas of what you had in mind when you wrote the text.

Below is the press release I wrote for a client whose book I edited. It will give you a little information about the book. Then following it is the two-sid-ed sell sheet I wrote the text for and Larry designed.

Press Release

Silicon Valley Exec Reveals How to Transform Employees into Innovators in New Book

January 6, 2014—Aviva Publishing, NY, today announced the release of Silicon Valley executive Jag Randhawa's new book *The Bright Idea Box*. This step-by-step guide teaches readers how to create a bottom-up innovation program, in which employees generate ideas to improve business processes, increase customer satisfaction, reduce operational costs, and raise the top line.

The book's thesis is simple, yet powerful: All employees have an innate desire to contribute to something bigger than themselves, beyond their ev-eryday job activities. *The Bright Idea Box* reveals how to tap into that desire by creating a platform that encourages employees to generate new ideas to benefit the business.

Some of the world's most innovative and successful companies, includ-ing Apple, Google, 3M, Toyota, and P&G, actively engage their employees to come up with new ideas to help grow the business. "Employees know the company products, processes, and the customers," said Randhawa. "They also have ideas for improving them, but they rarely have the means and a safe environment to voice them."

The Bright Idea Box introduces a six-step MASTER innovation program for employees to submit, develop, and implement ideas. MASTER is an acro-nym for the six steps. Randhawa walks the reader through each of the steps, including **Mobilize** (Creating the program's mission and objectives) and **Tri-age** (Creating a committee responsible for screening and prioritizing ideas).

Endorsements for *The Bright Idea Box*

Fellow business authors and experts are praising Randhawa's book and program. Daniel H. Pink, author of *TO SELL IS HUMAN* and *DRIVE* says, "*The Bright Idea Box* is part inspiration, part workbook, part resource, and a book everyone can learn from." Brian Tracy, author of *Full Engagement*, states, "This powerful, practical book shows you how to motivate, inspire, and get the very best out of each person in your company." And Marshall Goldsmith, named America's Preeminent Executive Coach by *Fast Company* magazine, proclaims, "*The Bright Idea Box* teaches you how to create practical, viable programs that will transform the company and the bottom line!"

About the Author

Jag Randhawa is a technology executive, professional speaker, executive coach, and corporate consultant. He has more than twenty years of technology industry experience with a strong track record of building high-performance teams and award-winning products. Born in India, Randhawa lives in the San Francisco Bay area with his wife, a neuroscientist, and two daughters.

- *The Bright Idea Box: A Proven System to Drive Employee Engagement and Innovation* (ISBN 978-1-938686-81-8 (h); ISBN: 978-1-940984-06-3 (p); Aviva Publishing, 2014) is available through local and on-line bookstores and as an ebook. A complete press kit is available at www.TheBrightIdeaBox.com. Review copies available upon request. Contact: Jag Randhawa, Jag@IdeaEmployee.com, 650-305-9110.

###

YOUR LEADERSHIP BLUEPRINT FOR BUSINESS SUCCESS

The Bright
IDEA BOX

A Proven System to Drive
Employee Engagement and Innovation

Jag Randhawa

Discover How Employee Engagement and Innovation Can Revolutionize Your Business

What do Toyota and Google have in common?

An all-inclusive "culture of innovation," in which every employee is responsible for coming up with ideas to make the company more successful.

Do you want your employees to be responsible for innovation as well? Do you believe that is possible? It absolutely is possible, and in *The Bright Idea Box*, technology executive and corporate consultant, Jag Randhawa, will show you how.

Book details
Title: *The Bright Idea Box: A Proven System to Drive Employee Engagement and Innovation*
List: $26.95 (hardcover), $19.95 (paperback)
Publishing Imprint: Aviva Publishing, N.Y.
Publication Date: Jan 13, 2014
Distributor: Ingram Book Company
Format: Hardcover (978-1-938686-81-8), Softcover (978-1-940984-06-3)
Website: www.TheBrightIdeaBox.com

Jag Randhawa is a Technology Executive, Professional Speaker, Executive Coach, and Corporate Consultant. Jag has more than twenty years of technology industry experience with a strong track record of building high performance teams and award-winning products. He is the mastermind behind the MASTER innovation program and the founder of Idea Employee Labs, a technology and management consulting company. Born in India, Jag now lives in the San Francisco Bay area with his wife, a neuroscientist, and two daughters.

"This powerful, practical book shows you how to motivate, inspire, and get the very best out of each person in your company."
— Brian Tracy, Author of
Full Engagement

"Great ideas don't just happen. Good leaders create a purposeful environment where brilliant ideas are generated, captured, and implemented. *The Bright Idea Box* is part inspiration, part workbook, part resource, and a book everyone can learn from."
— Daniel H. Pink, Author of
To Sell Is Human
and *Drive*

YOUR LEADERSHIP BLUEPRINT FOR BUSINESS SUCCESS

The Bright
IDEA BOX

A Proven System to Drive
Employee Engagement and Innovation

Jag Randhawa

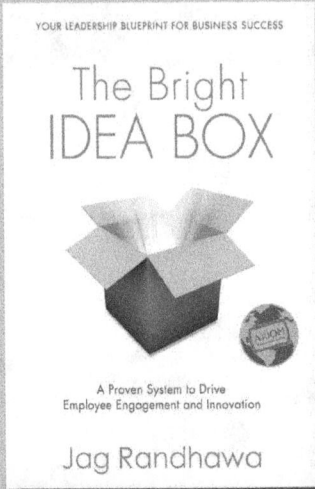

The Bright Idea Box introduces a six-step formula for creating a bottom-up innovation program. By reading this book, you will discover how introducing the Bright Idea Box program to your employees will:

- Encourage employees to generate ideas that add value to the company and customers
- Tap into employees' inner desires to do meaningful work, be part of something bigger, and be appreciated for their efforts
- Increase employee engagement, productivity, efficiencies, and customer satisfaction
- Create a stunning and lasting impact on your business performance

Begin to make it happen by reading *The Bright Idea Box.*

www.TheBrightIdeaBox.com

Praise for *The Bright Idea Box*

"Jag is one of those exceptional technologists, who demonstrate an exceptional understanding of people and how to motivate them to collaborate and excel. In this book, combining a timely synopsis of current management thought leadership and his own refinement and implementation of best practices, Jag provides a handbook for empowering employees, which leads to an explosion of engagement and innovation. This step-by-step guide is a valuable addition to any leader's library, providing insights into a possible, practical, and rewarding innovation process. A great return on your investment of time."
— Sophia Abramovitz, Program Management Executive, CEO, Norton Enterprises International, Inc.

"*The Bright Idea Box* provides readers with a simple secret "how-to" formula for employee engagement, plus dozens of invaluable tips, tricks, and techniques learned from many of the innovative giants in the marketplace, who put employee engagement and empowerment at the heart of their business models."
— Susan Friedmann, CSP, International Bestselling Author of *Riches in Niches: How to Make it BIG in a Small Market*

"If you are looking to reinvigorate your workforce to achieve your organizational goals, this book is the most important resource to help you get maximum results!"
— Patrick Snow, International Best Selling Author of *Creating Your Own Destiny* and *The Affluent Entrepreneur*

"More and more organizational leaders are realizing that the most efficient and effective way to stimulate growth is to engage the existing workforce and cultivate innovation from within. Jag Randhawa's *The Bright Idea Box* teaches you how to create practical, viable programs that will transform the company and the bottom line!"
— Marshall Goldsmith, America's Preeminent Executive Coach (*Fast Company* magazine)

"It is almost a no-brainer to read this book to MASTER six steps for creating a bottom-up innovation program that not only retains your best employees but engages them to provide meaningful contributions to business growth. Not-put-downable from cover-to-cover, forcing you to reach for your yellow highlighter at every page."
— Anurag Agrawal, CEO, Techaisle

Conclusion

You will likely be asked to look at or edit other marketing pieces, such as book markers, brochures, and letters written to sell the book to a publisher or literary agent if authors want to try to go the traditional publishing route.

It is not always easy to know what to charge for your time when helping with these projects. If I get a bookmarker from a client who just wants me to proofread it, it will likely take me less than five minutes, so I don't charge anything, and I am happy to help one of my clients succeed. If authors want you to edit or write marketing pieces on a regular basis, let them know your hourly rate and that you will keep a tab. Then ask authors to pay you when you reach a certain agreed-upon amount—$100 or $500 or whatever the two of you are comfortable with—or to pay you at the end of each month. I find it's best to be flexible with clients in these matters and also to make decisions on an individual basis according to what you have time to do, how trustworthy the client is, and whether you want to do the extra work.

Also, be forewarned that authors will often want you to help with a few things as they launch their books (or the careers those books are meant to support), such as editing a weekly blog post. I've found that authors who want to blog will start out strong and send you a blog regularly for about six weeks or so, but then soon they only send you one every few weeks, and after a few months, you no longer hear from them. If you're keeping a running tab for such authors, review your accounts at least once per year and request payment from everyone who still owes you money or you'll end up doing work you'll never get paid for.

Helping with these lesser marketing pieces can be a bit of a distraction from your main work if you have sufficient work, but you'll also find that in slow times, you are thankful for the extra money you get from clients who wanted you to write press releases and edit a few blog posts.

Chapter 15
Experiencing Abundance: Growing Your Business Beyond You

"Only those who will risk going too far
can possibly find out how far one can go."

— T. S. Eliot

As I STATED earlier, a lot of people out there want to be editors or are pretending to be editors even though they are not really qualified. I receive several requests a year from people who want editing work and want to work for me. These editors generally don't know how to find work for themselves. In truth, there is no lack of work out there; there is plenty to go around for everyone. Every year, more and more books are published. One study I read showed 2.2 million books were published worldwide in 2013, and 304,000 of those were in the United States. According to Bowker, in 2016, there were more than 700,000 books self-published in the United States alone. That's more than double within three years. Because of the self-publishing revolution, the number of books published per year just keeps growing and the number of editors, while probably also growing, is unlikely to keep up with it.

Really good editors have no lack of work. Their clients are happy with the work they do, so they keep coming back and referring all of their friends. Other editors may struggle to find enough work because their clients weren't happy with their work, they have poor communication and customer service skills, they don't turn around the work in a timely manner, or they simply don't know how to promote themselves.

As an editor, no matter how good you are, at least in the beginning, you can't expect work to come to you. You have to go out and find it through networking, joining author and editor associations, and not being afraid to tell everyone you meet what you do—and how you can help them when they confess they've always wanted to write a book.

Finding Help

After about three years of full-time editing, I had gotten so busy I needed help. I enlisted Larry because I knew he had the right skills. He had worked in the corporate world for twelve years, writing and editing a range of documents and publications and developing his web design and print layout skills in various training development and marketing positions. Larry was already building my websites and laying out my books, so that and managing a newspaper had given him some knowledge of the book publishing industry—not that books use a web press or have a weekly deadline, but there is some overlap. He also had been my office mate in graduate school when we were earning our master's degrees in English, so I knew first-hand he had strong writing skills and a critical eye for others' writing that was spot on when it came to what needed to be fixed.

At first, I just asked Larry to do a first edit of a book that was nearly incomprehensible and I didn't have time to do. All the sentences needed to be rewritten so they could make sense. He agreed to do it, and when he had finished, I did the second edit. After Larry smoothed out the sentences, I could focus on the book's content and organization and do the developmental editing the book needed.

Since then, I have regularly sent Larry books for the first edit. These are often roughly written or by authors for whom English is their second or third language. Larry doesn't usually do content editing, but sticks to line editing, figuring out what authors are trying to say and then rewording it so it is comprehensible. He also gives me a list of changes he thinks should be made to the book's content. Then I go in and fix the global issues (rearranging paragraphs and even chapters, writing in transitions, writing suggestions for development). By having Larry do the first edit, which usually takes twice as long as a second edit, I am able to save a lot of time that I can devote to editing other books without getting backed up.

That doesn't mean I only give Larry the worst of the work, however. His experience in the corporate world, especially the training courses he took advantage of while working for an international training development company, gave him the background to understand and translate engineer-speak, government regulations, and bad writing of all kinds into plain English. Sometimes, I also feel he is more knowledgeable about a topic than me. For example, if a book is about lean manufacturing, I might give it to him for the first edit because I know almost nothing about the subject. If the book is a business book that is more technical in nature, I feel he's a good resource to do the first edit, not only so he can smooth out the sentences, but also so he can give me suggestions for where more information is needed, or something doesn't make sense, etc. Then I either leave his comments in the manuscript for the author or I reword the section—sometimes I can figure out what the author is trying to say even if Larry can't or vice-versa.

At other times, I ask Larry to proofread a book because I feel I've spent so much time working on it that I'm not likely to catch errors or sections readers might still have difficulty understanding. I am always surprised and grateful for what Larry catches. A traditional publisher will often have two or three people edit and proofread a book, so by having a colleague who can help with the editing, I can ensure a better final product for authors. Three sets of eyes (including the author's) is always better than two, so it has become common for Larry and me both to go through almost every book.

Don't make finding help complicated. Fortunately, I had a friend I knew I could trust and who had the skills to help me, and Larry was happy to earn some extra money on the side. After a few years, we had enough business that he transitioned into working with me as his primary source of income. You may very likely have your own connections—friends whom you know from school or work who have the qualifications to do the job and help you. If you don't, don't worry too much. You probably will have people asking to work for or with you anyway, so you can pick and choose.

Here are a few pointers before you find someone to help you:

1. Make an agreement on the payment terms. Larry is not my employee. Since he was already doing my websites and book layout, he was working for himself. We decided to merge his website and mine so my clients would also go to him for layout and website work after I edited their books. We refer to each other as business colleagues to our clients, and we simply have an agreement that I will pay him so much for his work. He is basically a contract worker, so when I get a book in from a client that I want Larry to help with, I send the book to him, ask him to give me an estimate for the first edit, and then, once the client accepts the quote and Larry does the work, I pay him for those hours. Note that I pay him fewer dollars per hour than I charge the client because I need to make a small profit off his work, and I also will be doing work on the book after he is done. At the end of the month, I send Larry a check for whatever work he did. This way, I do not have to pay him an hourly wage for part-time or full-time work based on a set number of hours per week, and I don't have to pay any employee benefits. I just send him a 1099 form when tax season comes around showing how much I paid him for the year, just like I would anyone else I hired to do work for me.

2. Do not hire people solely because they are a friend or relative. It's often said never to go into business with a friend because it will lead to the end of the friendship. That may be true, but Larry and I have maintained our friendship and professional relationship for many years. That's not to say we haven't had our tense moments. Sometimes he has complained that there hasn't been enough work. Sometimes I've complained when he hasn't gotten a job done as quickly as I wanted. But overall, we both trust each other and know the other is loyal to the relationship and doing the best he can to get the work done quickly and accurately. We have been friends for a quarter of a century, but I did not hire him because he was my friend. I hired him because I knew he had the skills to do the job, and I knew I could trust him.

By comparison, I once had an acquaintance say to me, "Why don't you hire me? I can read." As if editing a book were that simple. I knew this person didn't have the skills to do the job and wouldn't be open to criticism during the training process. So don't hire someone just to be nice; doing so probably isn't being nice to yourself because it will lead to headaches later. And if you do hire someone and things aren't working out, don't be afraid to end the professional relationship with that person.

I certainly agree that in most cases it is better not to hire relatives or friends, but if you are certain you can trust them and will enjoy working with them, then wouldn't that be more fun than hiring strangers who may put on a good front when you hire them but could turn out to have issues you can't begin to guess at when you first begin working together?

Making Difficult Decisions

As my business has continued to grow, Larry and I have both become busier. That has resulted in some hard decisions. In some cases, I have had to decide to quit doing some of the things I did in the beginning. When I first became an editor, I did proofreading for a local magazine. It was a great way to polish my skills and see how others worked, and I enjoyed doing it. I also loved the people I worked with. What I didn't love was that it required me to work evenings after I had already put in a full day of work at home and that I had to drive to the magazine's office at night. I kept this job for too long because I felt I was needed there, and I had the mindset that things might fall apart if I didn't stay. No one is that valuable, and that magazine has done just fine since I left. I simply could not continue to work that many hours a week, so in the end, I had to let the job go. It was that or turn away some of my editing clients, and I was being paid significantly less at the magazine than what I was making editing books, so the decision became a no-brainer.

You may also have to make hard decisions about what you want to keep doing. For example, you might be editing full-length books as well as blog posts and shorter pieces for multiple clients. Eventually, you may need to downsize, or rather, become more focused on your top priorities and say no to clients who want things you no longer want to work on.

You don't always have to say no, however. You can sub-contract some of this work by hiring someone who will do it for less than the client is comfortable paying and you can then still make a small profit off it. If you hire someone to edit your client's blog posts for $25 an hour when you are charging $50, you've found a winner. You can make a profit off the work, keep the client happy, and provide work for someone else.

Now note, those numbers are just examples. I encourage you to pay your workers a fair and living wage for their work, but also take into consideration the person's experience and the fact that you deserve something for the effort you're putting into maintaining a relationship with the client and finding work for the other person. (You also have to be prepared to step in and do the work if the person working for you is sick or just quits unexpectedly.) I know many English majors who end up being teachers or working for a newspaper for much less than $25 an hour, so they would be happy to do some extra work on the side for that price. Most of these people will keep their day jobs and just supplement their income, which is great because they won't be expecting you to provide enough work to support them. As long as they're reliable and can turn-around the work in the time frame your client needs, you're all set.

Remember, it's your business, so don't babysit the people working for you or find yourself in a situation where you're basically running a charity. After years of managing a call center, the last thing I ever wanted was to have employees. Technically, the people I send work to do not work for me and are not my employees, so if someone isn't doing a good job, I can just send the work elsewhere.

Bottom line, as an editor, you can decide whether to turn work away or find reliable and qualified people to help you with the overflow—and make a profit off the work they do. If you think it's wrong to make a profit off someone else's work or not pay them the same as you, that's a noble idea, but not realistic. Every business with employees charges enough to pay said employees and still make a profit. Finding work for other people is not a hobby. You have to pay for your time securing the work. You have to think about your own nest egg and ensure you are financially stable before you can take care of the people working for you. If you try to do it the other way, you will stress yourself out trying to pay your bills, and you will not have the energy to run your business. Soon your clients will be unhappy, your contract workers will be taking advantage of you or leaving, and you'll give up and starve or go work for someone else—and trust me, once you've worked for yourself, you'll never want to work for someone else again.

Now that you understand the need for help, let's look at how you will manage the work and the people working under you so everyone is happy.

Being a Managing Editor

What exactly does being a managing editor entail? It means you primarily deal with your clients by email or phone, while the people who work for you do the work.

I admit managing is not as fun as editing if editing is what you love to do, but you can't do it all, and since you're going to be the mastermind of the business, you will need to wear the manager cap if you want your business to grow. You can either grow it, or you can turn clients away. If you love editing books and that's all you want to do, and you're making enough money to live on, you may not want to be a manager or outsource work to other editors. Guess what? That's fine, and I completely understand that. Some of us are workers and some of us are managers. That said, you've been managing projects for your editing clients anyway, so why not go the extra mile for them, and most importantly, for yourself, by finding people who can help you help your clients create the best books possible?

Let's say you have two editors and a layout person working under you. When a book comes in that needs editing, you give it to the editor you think is best for it, or who is open to take on the next book. That person might be you or it might be one of the other two editors.

If it's another editor, ask that editor to do an edit sample of the book and then come up with a price for doing the work. Then you will want to do an edit sample too to ensure the price is reasonable. Then mark up the other editor's price a little to cover your time managing the project. You also then want to add in the time you will need to proofread the book. Depending on how busy you are and how good you believe your editors are, you may want to let another editor always do a first edit of a book while you do the second edit. When authors send back revisions, you could have one of the editors go through the revisions to check them for grammar and punctuation, and then you can proofread the book, or you can have one of the other editors do the proofreading for you. Even if you have someone else do the proofreading, have that person turn on the track changes so you and the author can see the final changes made and you can double-check them.

I would recommend that, as the managing editor, you always do the proofreading or at least review changes made by the proofreader. That way you are performing the equivalent of a quality check before the book is laid out and printed to ensure your client will be happy and the people working under you are doing their jobs properly. If not, spend time training them— refer them to the style manual you made for your company or re-edit pieces they did to show them what more they could do. It's better to do this upfront than let other editors slack off in their work or do less than stellar work you have to redo, which wastes your time and money.

Delegating which editor will do which edit or proofread will be a juggling act if you have more than one person working for you, but I think it's better to juggle who does what with each individual project than to have one person do one thing every time and then have your workflow become bogged down because your team is waiting on one person to finish a task. As the managing editor, it's your job to keep the work in perpetual flow so everyone has work as often as possible and so the clients' books are completed in as speedy and accurate a manner as possible.

As I noted, you may also have a layout person working for you. The layout person will also need to bid on the job once the editing is completed. You will want to stay with your clients through the layout process and look over the proofs to ensure they meet your standards. You need to do this because layout people don't read the books they lay out; they will need help understanding what is really wanted, especially when it comes to reasons for indenting various items or levels of subtitles. Authors will also not know what to look for. Your job as managing editor is quality control of the book until it is printed.

As managing editor, you can also decide to what degree, if any, you will allow your editors and layout people to communicate with the client. It can be frustrating if you are in the middle, continually forwarding emails back and forth from clients, layout, and other editors when you are not as hands-on with the project and may not always know the details involved. However, you will be able to speak the language of everyone involved so you may be able to make things clear to all parties in a better way than they would be able to communicate to each other.

A danger also exists in letting your clients speak directly to sub-contractor editors or layout—authors may contact them directly when they want to start a new project, and your editors might end up doing work for them without your involvement, effectively taking business from you. In this situation, the client is also not getting your expertise or receiving the project's quality check. At times, clients may feel it's easier to talk directly to subordinate editors or layout, but you want to avoid this situation as much as possible. Once you have worked with your editors for a while, you will have a better sense of their loyalty to you, but you don't want to risk hiring an editor who is going to take your clients. I've never had this happen to me, but I know other business owners, both in the publishing industry and elsewhere, who have had this happen.

No hard and fast rules exist for setting up your business' workflow when other people work under you. It will require some trial and error in the beginning. As time goes by, you'll learn your fellow editors' strengths and weaknesses, and then you'll be better able to judge who should do a first edit, a second edit, or a proofread; who would be better qualified to edit a business book or romance novel; and who is better at guessing what an author who learned English as a second language is trying to say.

Structure your business in whatever way is most comfortable for you. And make sure you have fun with it. If one of your editors isn't working out—not doing high quality work or not meeting deadlines—let that person go. If a project doesn't feel right for you and your group, let the project go. If you feel like you should do the second edit and can trust someone else to do the proofreading, that's preferable (provided you review the changes the proofreader made). As long as your gut feels good about everything, you're likely doing fine, but if something doesn't feel good to you, I can assure you that you need to stop doing whatever it is before it gets worse. Do not frustrate yourself by trying to control people or situations that are out of your control. End the situation by firing the client or the contract worker, and move on.

When all else fails, turn the situation over to your Higher Power (which may be God, Buddha, Jesus, Allah, the Universe, or whatever term you feel comfortable with). My late friend, Irene Watson, who owned Reader Views and for whom I did a lot of contract work in the beginning of my editing career, named herself the managing editor of her company, but she always said God was the CEO. You may not be a religious person, but if you believe in any sort of Higher Power, then when something isn't working out, turn it over to your Higher Power and look deeply into your heart for your Higher Power's answer. Once you receive the answer, act on it. Never forget that you are working for yourself so you can work for yourself. It is your life and your business, so you get to decide how it will play out. Don't let anyone rain on your parade or ruin your day. Life is too short. With help from your Higher Power, you can make the best decisions for you and your business.

Creating Your All-Star Team

So you've decided you have too much work to do yourself, but you don't want to turn people away. You want someone to help you. But how do you find the right person? And if you keep growing, how many people will you need?

I initially got lucky. As I stated earlier, Larry was qualified and also available to help me. That doesn't mean that in the beginning we didn't have a few issues. I would send him work to do and sometimes he would not catch things I would have fixed. (Of course, I was always embarrassed by what he caught that I missed when he proofread.) Over time, I would have him do a first edit and then I would do the second edit and send it back to him so he could see what I changed that he might have missed. (Of course, no one is going to fix everything that needs fixing in a book on the first read-through so he was bound to miss a few things.) But I was also able to point out certain things I caught that he repeatedly wasn't catching, such as maybe not fixing subject-pronoun agreement, until in time we were both on the same page. Ultimately, this process led to my creating our company style guide. In some cases, Larry would disagree with me about the proper way to do something, and after consideration and researching it, I would accept that he was right and agree to change how we did it. I always had the ultimate say, since I was paying him, but I was open to learning from him, and you need to do the same when working with the people you hire. You always want people who are as smart and knowledgeable, or even smarter and more knowledgeable, working for you. As I said, I was fortunate in that regard.

Other Editors: The first person you'll want on your team is another editor, and in time, maybe several. You may already know someone who can help you, but it doesn't hurt to advertise for someone. I would not recommend taking out an ad in the newspaper or sending a message to all your Facebook friends, but you likely have connections with other editors, and you likely will have the occasional editor contact you looking for work. If you don't know anyone else, then go on Facebook, LinkedIn, or work-related sites to see other editors' profiles or google editors and visit their websites. If people ask whether they can work for you, ask them to send you their resumes and samples of their writing or editing, and then when you have extra work, you can consider them.

Don't hire anyone without seeing editing samples. Better yet, ask the prospective editor to do new sample edits. Choose a few pages from different clients you've worked with. (I always keep the various drafts of all the manuscripts I've edited, so if you do the same, it won't be hard to find some samples.) Send a few original pages from a manuscript or two to prospective editors with the track changes feature turned on so you'll be able to see what changes are made. (It's important to maintain your clients' anonymity and confidentiality, so don't send pages with names or any revealing information on them about your clients.) When prospective editors send back the edited samples, go over them carefully to see what they changed and also missed. (You may even have your original edit sample from the book so you can compare it to other editors' work.) Then you can decide whether prospective editors are qualified to work with you.

When prospective editors do the edit sample, also ask them to time themselves and let you know how long it took. Explain that it is imperative they be honest about how long it takes, since if they claim it took less time than it did, they will be shortchanging themselves down the road. (I'll explain more about the importance of timing below when we discuss negotiating a wage.)

You can also make up a quiz for prospective editors to take. It could be multiple choice, such as "Which of these three sentences is correctly punctuated?" You could also write a short essay yourself with intentional errors in it. Tell prospects there are twenty errors in the one-page essay and they need to correct them all. If they get them all, great. If not, you can decide, based on how many they did fix, whether they are someone you want to work with and whether you can train them to spot all the issues and correct them. You might even be surprised to find that they catch something you didn't mean to mess up, which is even better. After all, none of us is perfect. That's why it's always good to have an extra pair of eyes look at our work.

Be sure you also interview prospects over the phone or in person. If they have never done editing before, ask questions about their educations, why they want to be editors, and what their future plans are. If they have editing experience, ask specific questions, such as about their favorite types of books to edit, their best and worst editing experiences, and their opinions on language-specific items, such as subject-pronoun agreement, split infinitives, or anything else that concerns you. In all these cases, while you want the right answers—or educated ones, since some of these matters are debatable—what's most important is that you feel you are on the same page and your personalities are compatible.

Once you decide you want to work with someone, you can negotiate a fair hourly wage. Before you discuss money, look at the changes in the edit samples and the time it took to do them to get an idea of how fast the person edits. Track changes has a time stamp, so you can use that to verify durations (provided you check within twenty-fours; after that, track changes will just say the day of the week the changes were made.). If someone can edit 4,000 words an hour, that's better than 2,000, but, of course, those numbers will vary depending on the level of difficulty required with each editing project. (People may also take longer than normal doing the edit samples because they want to be super-careful to catch everything, so keep that in mind. Accuracy is more important than speed. You'll be able to tell from the track changes how long it took so you'll also know whether the person was honest with you about it.)

You want to establish an hourly wage you and prospective editors can agree upon, but you do not want to pay hourly. The reason is if you give clients a price and assume your editor can do the first edit in twenty hours, and it ends up taking thirty, you either have to ask the client for more money (never a good idea) or you have to pay the editor out of your own pocket (which won't make you happy). As a result, you want the editors working for you to become good at coming up with accurate bids. Let's say you agree to pay editors $25 an hour and they believe the project will take twenty hours. That's $500. If an editor ends up doing $750 worth of work, you're still going to pay $500 because that's what you agreed on and, consequently, that was worked into the price the client paid. The editor will then learn to bid more accurately on the next job. Of course, extenuating circumstances may arise, in which case you may have to ask the author for more money or agree to pay the editor extra out of your pocket—but that is also why, when you take the editor's bid and add it to your own costs for the work you will do proofreading and managing the project, you inflate slightly to create a pricing cushion for anything unexpected. And trust me, the unexpected often arises—usually, it has to do with how much attention clients need, but it could also have to do with the manuscript's quality.

Occasionally, no matter what you do, you are going to have jobs where you will put in more hours than you estimated. That's the nature of the game, but as time goes by, you and those who work under you will learn how to quote more accurately.

Layout People/Cover Designers: You may choose to have layout people work under you also, or you can simply refer authors to them so you don't have to pay them directly, and then ask them to pay you a referral fee. As stated previously, a reasonable referral fee is 10 percent, so if you've edited a book and then you refer the author to a layout person, have an agreement with the layout person that you get 10 percent for the referral. The layout person will then create a quote for the client that includes the referral fee. The author doesn't need to know about your referral fee agreement, but this way you are paid for your time trying to convince the author to hire the layout person and for finding a reliable layout person for the author. You'll also be looking over the proofs (time you already added to your initial price).

Sometimes, authors will ask me to recommend a layout person; other times, they already have someone. They will often then ask me if it matters to me which layout person they hire. I always say no and leave it up to the author, but if you can get the author to use the layout person you have agreements with, you're better off. You're also better off because you and the layout person have developed a relationship over time and know how to communicate with each other. Several times in my experience when an author has had a layout person already in mind, that person has turned out not to be a layout person but someone the author knows who does graphic design and doesn't know much about books. As a result, I have to spend more time working with this layout person to make sure things look the way they should. I've worked with layout people who have laid out a book without putting any headers or page numbers in it. I've even seen a so-called cover designer not put the author's name on the front cover. I can be patient, but having to teach layout people how to do their job takes up more of my time, so I recommend you find a couple of layout people you can refer all your editing clients to whom you can establish good relationships with and who are willing to pay you referral fees.

Other Services for Referral: You may also want to establish referral fee agreements with other people in the book industry. Your clients will actually appreciate this because finding an editor is usually the first thing they do, and they don't know where to go from there, so if you can also act like a publishing coach for them by sending them on to other services, they will appreciate that as well. Other services may include:

- Cover designers
- Indexers
- Book reviewers/bloggers

- Printers
- Website designers
- Book video creators
- Graphic designers who do marketing pieces
- Speaking coaches

Many of the people who do these jobs overlap with others. For example, most layout people have graphic design backgrounds so they will do both covers and interior layout, and they might also do websites or be willing to create brochures, business cards, sell sheets, etc. for authors. Start with finding a good book layout person. If this person has the skills to provide these services as well, that's great. If not, find some people who can.

The more people you have to refer your clients to, the better for you and the better for your clients because you will be sending them to your friends in the publishing business—reputable people whom you know will do a good job for your clients. There are several sharks in the publishing world, so do your best to steer your clients clear of them. By sharks, I mean people who are posing as editors, layout designers, website designers, etc. but who have minimal or no qualifications and are interested in making a quick buck but not in making clients happy.

Remember, you are primarily providing a service to your clients; any business you can pass on to industry friends is great, but ultimately, while you want to help others, you have to help yourself first. Don't be ashamed of getting referral fees or making a profit off the editors and other people working under you. Without you, those people might not have work at all. Practice an attitude of gratitude every day—gratitude that you have work, gratitude that you have clients, and gratitude that you have loyal workers you can trust to do high quality work for you and your clients. If you do your best every day and are grateful for what you have, the money will take care of itself.

Chapter 16
It's a Wonderful Life: Giving Back

"To write is human, to edit is divine."

— Stephen King

I'M A FIRM believer in abundance. As I mentioned early in this book, I have spent years studying and doing my best to learn how to use the Law of Attraction. Consequently, I believe there is plenty of work and money out there for everyone. You just have to learn how to attract it. Once you do, you become so excited about what you've learned that you want to share it with everyone.

I believe I have been successful for two reasons, neither of them having anything to do with luck. One reason is my determination and perseverance. The other is through following the Law of Attraction and believing in abundance. If you sit around worrying that you won't have enough work, you'll be negative and sound desperate when you talk to potential clients, which will scare them off. If you do your best to help people and just trust the Universe will provide, it will. I also believe in karma, so I know that what goes around comes around. In other words, I believe if I help people, it will come back to me multifold, so I do my best to help any author I can.

Giving While Beginning Your Business

I decided to write this book because I know a lot of people want to become editors but don't know how to go about it. I see no reason to keep my secrets to myself—and they really aren't secrets so much as just advice based in experience, motivation, and knowledge of the publishing industry. I hope this book has helped you, and in turn, that you will help others. Nothing is more rewarding than when you help someone and then see that person shine and go forward to make a difference in the world.

Don't wait until you're making a six-figure income to start helping people. Do it right from the beginning. When you are beginning your business and looking for editing clients, you have a perfect opportunity to volunteer to help others, helping yourself in the process. Join a committee at your church or at a non-profit and volunteer to be the newsletter editor or to write fundraising letters or whatever writing/editing is needed. That way, you'll be using your writing and editing skills and you'll also be making other people aware of them. Usually, people who are on boards have a lot of connections in the community, including among business owners. A good word from the right person about your talents could help you find a lifetime of business.

Mentoring Others

Once you're established as an editor, be willing to help others develop their skills. There is so much work out there—the number of books published each year, as I noted earlier, just keeps increasing—so don't worry that someone will steal your clients. Editing is a global business. It's not like you have only the people in your town to serve and if someone sets up shop next-door to you, you might have to close. You'll have clients locally, certainly, but you'll also find clients all over the country, and even the world, if you make an effort to promote yourself and do a good job so clients refer you to all of their friends.

If people express interest in becoming an editor, spend an hour talking to them about how you did it (and recommend this book). For all you know, these people might be great resources for you once they get established. They might overflow work to you and vice-versa. You might not like to edit science fiction novels, but now you'll know someone who does to whom you can refer clients. Those clients will appreciate your honesty, and if you tell them your specialty is romance novels, then they'll send their romance novelist friends to you. More importantly, your editing mentee will send those clients to you also. You might even want to take these newbie editors under your wing and let them do an apprenticeship or internship with you to help them polish their skills while lightening your workload.

Giving Without Over-Giving

Once you become successful, you may find you have limited free time. To be honest, I tend to get stressed out when I have too much work, but somehow I always manage to get it all done, and I usually get it done sooner than I expected. As time goes by, you'll learn how to balance your work and personal life so you can cope with your stress. That said, there are only so many hours in a day, and you can't help everyone.

I talked earlier about turning away projects that aren't right for you. Again, you also need to know how to set boundaries. I often have people who want me to go out for lunch to talk to them about book publishing. In some cases, these people will end up being clients. Sometimes they do not. Here's how I handle this situation so I do not end up wasting my time. If authors have a completed manuscript, I ask them to email it to me so I can look it over and do an edit sample. I tell them that after I do that, I'll be in a better position to talk about the book and give effective advice. I usually find that once I do this and give authors a price quote, they are usually satisfied and hire me—and a meeting becomes unnecessary. Many authors simply think a meeting is the way to begin the process, and I'm all for having a friendly meeting with people if I have time, but most of what needs to be done can be handled by email or phone. If authors don't have a completed manuscript but are only in the middle of writing a book or thinking about writing a book, I invite them to come to our local author organization's monthly or annual meeting to learn more about the book publishing industry. Sometimes, I also refer authors to other authors or editors if they are not writing books I feel comfortable editing.

All that said, don't be so stringent about your time that if an author is insistent in wanting to meet with you, you refuse. The author is still a potential client, and you always want to keep work coming in. Even authors who do not end up hiring you will likely remember you gave them advice and possibly refer other authors to you. You may also be delighted by people once you meet. Some might be fabulous writers, or even potential new friends, although you want to remain professional when it comes to working on clients' projects even if you become close friends.

You'll find that how your clients want to communicate with you will also have a lot to do with their generation. Baby boomers will almost always want to meet you in person if you live in the same area. If not, they will definitely be the ones who will call to talk to you on the phone. Generation X authors may call or email you initially to make contact, but after that, you are pretty safe assuming that your relationship will be largely through email with a phone call only when necessary. Millennials and some Gen Xers will want to text you. Personally, I dislike texting. I have big fingers and it takes me forever to write a text with proper punctuation and spelling. Yes, I know everyone texts today using texting language, but as the editor, you do not want typos in your texts, which will reflect poorly on you as a professional, and trust me, people love to make fun of editors' typos, so as much as possible I try to avoid texting, but if you're a whiz at it, do what works best for you.

Learn to communicate with your clients in the manner they prefer so long as it is also conducive to getting your work done. Try to be as efficient as possible, but don't be so stringent you can't meet a client for lunch or coffee if need be. If a client suggests lunch, ask whether you can meet for coffee instead. Then you don't have to wait for the food and the bill and can leave sooner if need be. I also recommend meeting in a public place rather than your home, not because the prospective client may be a psycho, but again, so you have some control over ending the meeting rather than having a client sitting on your sofa whom you don't want to be rude to and throw out, but who won't stop talking. Plus, you always want to project a professional attitude, and your home is not always conducive to that, especially if you have children and pets who might interrupt, other clients calling, or you just simply don't have time to keep your house as clean as you would like.

So give those free consultations to the clients who ask for them, but don't give so much of yourself that you don't have time to do the work that pays or have some time to yourself.

Offering Your Services to Causes You Believe In

Once you become successful, you will likely have a busy editing schedule that might not leave time for much else. Be firm with setting boundaries for yourself. Don't work twelve-hour days, plus weekends. I did that far too long until I read the *Workaholics Anonymous* book and learned how to be kind to myself. I have time set aside every day to exercise, read, watch TV, and do my own writing. I am very stringent about my work and my personal time, and while I make time for friends and family, I try not to let my personal life interfere with my work or vice-versa.

As you become known for your services, you will find that many people want a piece of your time. I am often asked to participate in various events in the community from being on boards to helping at charitable events. There are no hard rules on whether you should accept or refuse to participate in such activities other than to do what feels good for you. If you are asked to be on a board for an organization you care about and you feel the desire to serve, go ahead and do it. If being on a board isn't for you, offer to help in other ways. Planning a dinner reception is not for me, but I am happy to write a marketing piece for an event or to proofread a grant to help a cause I care about.

Remember that whatever you can do in the community may get you noticed. If you donate money to organizations, donate it in your company's name. Often, events and associations publish the names or company names of those who donate, so that is added publicity for your business. Don't forget that charitable donations are also a tax deduction.

You can give back in many ways. You are giving back just by helping to publish wonderful books that will make the world a better place, even if you are paid to do it. You are giving back when you give authors and wannabe editors information. You are giving back when you use your skills to support good causes.

Find ways to show your gratitude for what the Universe has given you, and the Universe will keep giving. It's a wonderful life when you let it be.

A Final Note

"People who succeed have momentum. The more they succeed, the more
they want to succeed, and the more they find a way to succeed."

— Tony Robbins

OW YOU KNOW how to become a nomadic freelance editor and how
to keep business coming in so you're set for the long run. The
question is: After everything you've read, is being an editor the
ideal job for you?

If the answer is yes, let me caution you now not to quit your day job.
Instead, advertise your editing services and start working on your business
part-time. This might mean you have to turn down an occasional editing
job because you don't have time to do it as quickly as your client requires. It
also means you will have to work some long hours, including weekends and
evenings. Do not let your editing side job compromise your work at your day
job. Don't try editing books at the office when you're supposed to be focused
on other things. Also, do not lose sleep, staying up half the night to edit.
When you get so busy that you have no personal life, then you'll know you're
ready to take the leap and become a full-time editor. Then you can leave your
day job.

But don't leap blindly. Establish your emergency fund before you leave
your day job so you're prepared when work is slow. When I left my day job,
I was lucky because I had several weeks' worth of vacation saved up that the
company paid me for, which helped a lot. If possible, ask your boss if you can
work part-time or go out and find a part-time job to free up some more time
for your editing business while still providing some stable income.

Perhaps most importantly, don't be afraid to tell everyone you're an editor. Tons of people have books in them and are just aching to figure out how

to write a book or how to get that manuscript into a printed form. Help them all you can. Go the extra mile for people, and they'll go the extra mile in referring future clients to you.

I know this system works because it's the system I used myself, but I also know that everyone is not as dedicated as me or loves playing with words all day like I do. Begin slowly and test the waters. In time, you'll know whether you have what it takes to be a freelance editor.

I wish you much happiness on your editing journey. If I can help you in any way, my contact information can be found on the following pages.

Here's to your success!

Tyler R. Tichelaar

Resources

Books on Writing and Editing

Borel, Brooke. *The Chicago Guide to Fact-Checking.* Chicago, IL: U of Chicago P, 2016.

Chiarella, Tom. *Writing Dialogue: How to Create Memorable Voices and Fictional Conversations that Crackle with Wit, Tension and Nuance.* Cincinnati, OH: Story Press, 1998.

Dunham, Steve. *The Editor's Companion: An Indispensable Guide to Editing Books, Magazines, Online Publications, and More.* Blue Ash, OH: Writer's Digest Books, 2015.

Einsohn, Amy. *The Copyeditor's Handbook: A Guide for Book Publishing and Corporate Communications.* 3rd ed. Chicago, IL: U of Chicago P, 2011.

Forster, E. M. *Aspects of the Novel.* 1927. New York, NY: Harcourt, n.d.

Ginna, Peter. *What Editors Do: The Art, Craft, and Business of Book Editing.* Chicago, IL: U of Chicago P, 2017.

Hamilton, Carolyn V. *Power Editing for Fiction Writers.* Las Vegas, NV: Swift House Press, 2015.

Hough, John Jr. *The Fiction Writer's Guide to Dialogue: A Fresh Look at an Essential Ingredient of the Craft.* New York, NY: Allworth Press, 2015.

Howard-Johnson, Carolyn. *The Frugal Editor: Do-It-Yourself Editing Secrets for Authors: From Your Query Letter to Final Manuscript to the Marketing of Your Bestseller.* 2007. 2nd ed. CreateSpace, 2015.

King, Stephen. *On Writing: A Memoir of the Craft.* New York, NY: Pocket Books, 2001.

Leonard, Elmore. *Ten Rules on Writing.* New York: William Morrow, 2007.

Michener, James A. *James A. Michener's Writer's Handbook: Explorations in Writing and Publishing.* New York, NY: Dial Press, 1992.

Norton, Scott. *Developmental Editing: A Handbook for Freelancers, Authors, and Publishers*. Chicago, IL: U of Chicago P, 2009.

Saller, Carol Fisher. *The Subversive Copy Editor: Advice from Chicago (or, How to Negotiate Good Relationships with your Writers, Your Colleagues, and…Guides to Writing, Editing, and Publishing)*. 2nd ed. Chicago, IL: U of Chicago P, 2016.

Rand, Ayn. *The Art of Fiction: A Guide for Writers and Readers*. New York, NY: Penguin, 2000.

Rand, Ayn. *The Art of Nonfiction: A Guide for Writers and Readers*. New York, NY: Penguin, 2000.

Strunk, William. *The Elements of Style*. Amazon Digital Services: 2011. (Free as a Kindle ebook)

Zisner, William. *On Writing Well, 30th Anniversary Edition: An Informal Guide to Writing Nonfiction*. New York, NY: Harper Perennial, 2012.

Books on Publishing, Marketing, and Business

Ferriss, Timothy. *The 4-Hour Workweek: Expanded and Updated*. New York, NY: Random House, 2009.

Kremer, John. *1001 Ways to Market Your Books*. Taos, NM: Open Horizons, 2006.

Poynter, Dan. *Dan Poynter's Self-Publishing Manual: How to Write, Print and Sell Your Own Book (Volume 2)*. Santa Barbara, CA: Para Publishing, 2009.

Tichelaar, Tyler. *Creating a Local Historical Book: Fiction and Non-Fiction Genres*. Ann Arbor, MI: Modern History Press, 2012.

Watson, Irene, Tyler Tichelaar, and Victor Volkman, eds. *Authors Access: 30 Success Secrets for Authors and Publishers*. Ann Arbor, MI: Modern History Press, 2008.

Dictionaries

I've found that an online dictionary is far more efficient than a paper dictionary. But you never know when your internet connection might go down, so keep a good paper dictionary handy. I recommend the latest edition of Merriam-Webster for your paper copy. Below are my thoughts on online dictionaries.

Dictionary.com: I use Dictionary.com 99 percent of the time. It has excellent listings of definitions, plus dates for word origins, which is important if you are editing historical fiction. It also has a thesaurus, as do the sites listed below that I use on the rare occasion when I disagree with Dictionary.com.

English Oxford Dictionary: (https://en.oxforddictionaries.com/) A good resource for comparing British and American spellings. Also good for word origin and usage information.

Merriam-Webster Dictionary: (Merriam-Webster.com) Good for a second opinion if you strongly disagree with Dictionary.com, for example whether a word should be two words, one word, or hyphenated.

Urban Dictionary: (Urbandictionary.com) A good resource for slang and popular language usage that may not be in the standard dictionaries listed above.

Grammar Sources

English Simplified: Ellsworth, Blanche and John Higgins. *English Simplified*. 13th ed. New York, NY: Pearson, 2012. This is my all-time favorite grammar book. I have used it since 1991, both as a student and as a college composition instructor.

Grammar Girl: (http://www.quickanddirtytips.com/education/grammar) This website is a bit hard to navigate but just google the grammar issue you want information on and you'll find it. For example, search for "whom vs who grammar girl."

Grammarly: (grammarly.com) You can download this program to your computer. It is a grammar and spell-check program, but beyond its proofreading skills, it has plagiarism checking skills, which you'll find useful for those many authors who copy and paste whole articles and paragraphs into their books from the internet with no understanding that they need to cite the information.

Style Manuals

I recommend, when possible, subscribing to the online versions of style manuals to ensure you have timely information and updates. The online style manuals also make it easier to search for what you want compared to the somewhat convoluted indexes and contents pages in the manuals.

American Medical Association (AMA) Manual of Style: http://www.amamanualofstyle.com/

American Psychological Association (APA) Stylebook: (apastyle.org) Access to the online manual is only available to institutions, but you can order the current paper version from the website, plus some other helpful resources can be accessed at the site.

American Society of Mechanical Engineers (ASME): (https://www.asme.org) There is no actual style manual for engineers, but this site gives guidelines on formatting and citations for engineering papers.

Associated Press (AP) Stylebook: apstylebook.com

Chicago Manual of Style (CMOS): chicagomanualofstyle.org

Christian Writer's Manual of Style: (https://www.zondervan. com/9780310527909/the-christian-writers-manual-of-style/) Published by Zondervan, the Christian publisher. The manual is not available in an online version but can be purchased at the website.

Foreign Style Manuals: View the list at https://en.wikipedia.org/wiki/ List_of_style_guides

Turabian: https://www.chicagomanualofstyle.org/turabian/citation-guide. html

Additional Resources

Book Industry Study Group: View its listing of BISAC (genre) codes at www.bisg.org

Editorial Freelancers Association: https://www.the-efa.org/

WA World Services Organization. *Workaholics Anonymous Book of Recovery*. 2005. 3rd ed. Menlo Park, CA: Workaholics Anonymous World Services Organization, 2009.

Tyler Tichelaar in Ephesus, Turkey

About the Author

Tyler R. Tichelaar has a PhD in Literature from Western Michigan University, and bachelor and master's degrees in English from Northern Michigan University. He has taught various English courses from Freshman Composition to Argumentative Writing and the British Literature Surveys at Northern Michigan University, Western Michigan University, and Clemson University.

Tyler began writing his first novel when he was sixteen. After years of searching for a publisher, he decided to self-publish his novel *Iron Pioneers: The Marquette Trilogy, Book One* in 2006. Soon, other authors began to ask him for help with their own books. By joining the Upper Peninsula Publishers and Authors Association and various writing and publishing groups online, Tyler quickly began to make connections and soon was able to become a full-time freelance editor.

Today, Tyler operates his own editing company, Superior Book Productions, which has edited more than four hundred titles to date. Tyler also owns his own publishing company, Marquette Fiction. He is the author of numerous books, including The Marquette Trilogy, *My Marquette, Haunted Marquette, The Best Place, King Arthur's Children: A Study in Fiction and Tradition, The Gothic Wanderer: From Transgression to Redemption, When Teddy Came to Town*, and the five books of the Children of Arthur series. He has been the President of the Upper Peninsula Publishers and Authors Association for eleven years. For five years, he was guest co-host of the *Authors Access* internet radio show, and for ten years the book reviewer for *Marquette Monthly* as well as the proofreader for nine.

In 2009, Tyler won first place in the Reader Views Literary Awards in the historical fiction category for his novel *Narrow Lives*. He has since gone on to sponsor that award. In 2011, he received the Barb H. Kelly Historical Preservation Award from the Marquette Beautification and Restoration Committee for his book *My Marquette*. That same year, he was named the Outstanding Writer of the year in the Marquette County Arts Awards. In 2014, in partnership with the Marquette Regional History Center, he received a grant from the Michigan Humanities Council to produce his play *Willpower: An Original Play about Marquette's Ossified Man*.

A nomad at heart, Tyler loves to travel, especially to Europe, to learn more about history, meet interesting people, and do research for his books. As an avid genealogist, he has traced his ancestry to ancient times and has ancestors from every country in Europe and several in Asia and Africa, making him believe he is a true citizen of the world and that racial boundaries really do not exist.

Tyler is always happiest when he is editing, writing, researching, reviewing, or just plain reading a book. He is grateful that he can spend his life doing work he loves, and he delights in knowing that the books he helps birth go out into the world to make a difference to more people than anyone can ever count.

You can find out more about Tyler's books at his websites:

www.MarquetteFiction.com

www.ChildrenofArthur.com

www.GothicWanderer.com

Thank You for Reading *The Nomad Editor*

If you enjoyed this book, please consider writing a short book review at Amazon, Barnes & Noble, Goodreads, or another online bookseller's website. Book reviews are the best way, along with word-of-mouth, to help a book's sales and show your appreciation for the author's hard work. Even just a few words or a sentence or two can make a difference in helping an author.

Thank you, and best wishes with all your editing projects!

Tyler R. Tichelaar

Hire Tyler Tichelaar to Be Your Editing Coach

Do you want to be an editor, but you're not quite sure whether your skills are up to par?

If that's a concern for you, then you probably have what it takes to be an editor because you want to do high quality work.

Tyler Tichelaar can help you hone your skills so you are up-to-date with publishing industry standards and able to provide the professional services authors need.

If you hire Tyler as your editing coach, he will work with you on editing actual manuscripts from his clients. Tyler will walk you through a first edit, review your edits and point out what you may have missed, and also review your proofreading of the manuscripts. Working with Tyler is not just taking an editing test for certification. It is the equivalent to doing an internship with an experienced editor.

To find out more about hiring Tyler as your editing coach, email him to schedule a complimentary interview. Mention that you read his book, let him know what time zone you are in, tell him when the best date and time to talk would be, and mention any editing qualifications you may already have. He'll then schedule a free thirty- to sixty-minute interview with you.

Tyler@SuperiorBookProductions.com

Hire Superior Book Productions to Build Your Editor Website

Superior Book Productions built its own website, www.SuperiorBook-Productions.com, to promote its editing services, so let us now help you with your website.

Larry Alexander, website designer for Superior Book Productions, will help you design a simple—or complex, depending on your needs—website to promote your editing services so your clients know what you do and how you can help them.

We also design and build author websites. You can be sure we will take good care of your author friends.

Contact Larry today at:

Larry@SuperiorBookProductions.com

"Larry Alexander created the website for my book with artistic sensibility and technical know-how. The result is pages with stunning visual appeal and essential content that showcases my book and invites the reader to buy it. I definitely recommend him as your webmaster!"

— Marianne Campagna, author of *Reflections from Gavea*,
www.ReflectionsfromGavea.com

Earn Extra Money by Referring Authors to
Superior Book Productions

Even if you've decided that being an editor is not for you, you can still make money in the publishing industry by referring authors to Superior Book Productions. Send Tyler an email at Tyler@SuperiorBookProductions.com, letting him know you know several authors and will be referring them to Superior Book Productions to get their books edited. Superior Book Productions pays a 10 percent referral fee, so if you send us an author whose book ends up being a $1,500 edit job, you'll get $150 from us.

If you do become an editor, that's fabulous. We're happy this book could help put you on the road to rewarding work. Keep Superior Book Productions in mind, however, for book layout, website design, marketing pieces, ebook creation, or any of the other services we offer. We'll gladly pay you a referral fee for any client you refer who hires us.

For more information about all the services Superior Book Productions offers, visit us at:

www.SuperiorBookProductions.com

www.ingramcontent.com/pod-product-compliance
Lightning Source LLC
Chambersburg PA
CBHW060047100426
42742CB00014B/2732